*"As long as we view rape as seduction,
and at worst unwanted sex,
we will never understand rape."*

—Andrea Rechtin

dedication

Dedicated to Rev. Sydney A. Magill-Lindquist

This book is dedicated to my wife Sydney. Her constant love and undying support for me and this work is a testament to her faith in not only me, but to all women's right to be safe and free from fear, intimidation, and control. I can only wish that all men might have the good fortune and blessing of a partner who has always been in my corner...even when I wasn't.

acknowledgments

Thank you to all those who have made this book possible.

First, I would like to thank my agent, Barbara Levine. Without her initiative this book would never have found its rightful place with Sourcebooks.

One person has shaped and honed this book and fine-tuned my skills as a writer. That person is Deborah Werksman. If I am a good writer and if this book is accepted and lauded, it is because of her skills as an editor and supportive friend. Her commitment to this work is truly remarkable. She has taught me the importance of every word I write and reminded me that: "It's the message, not the messenger, that is important."

I would also like to take this opportunity to thank my mother-in-law, Eva Magill, who had faith in me and my work, even when she didn't quite understand all that I was doing.

My daughter Rachael taught me how to think and be young and how to reach other teenagers like herself as a friend and not as an overbearing and boring grown-up.

Finally, I want to thank all the many thousands of women and men who have taught me the realities of rape and dating communication. For all those survivors of rape, this book is for you and the courage you found to keep going and keep thriving. Your hope and faith in your ability to heal and be whole again has kept me going when I felt like giving up.

God bless you all.

table of contents

introduction

Since 1982, when I began my career as a crime prevention specialist, there has been a media trend focused on the related issues of rape, sexual assault, sexual harassment, and domestic violence. The question remains as to whether these problems have become worse, or whether more women are reporting them. There are many books, articles, and studies on the epidemic of sexual assault in the United States, most of which are statistical and address the issues after the fact—after the assault has taken place, after the violence has been committed. This book is about prevention.

The challenge facing this book is how to reach women at all stages of life about the realities of sexual assault without scaring them into denial. The mere mention of the word "rape" causes many people so much discomfort that they want either to ignore the problem or to pretend it doesn't exist. It is for this reason that I have tried to simplify stories and other related crime prevention information from the most reliable and up-to-date sources into a concise guidebook for preventing sexual assault in all its forms, with the emphasis on date/acquaintance rape.

This book will explore a number of dangerous situations in which a woman might find herself being sexually assaulted. These situations include date/acquaintance rape, which is the main focus of this book, as well as stranger rape, sexual harassment, stalking, dating violence, and domestic violence. These areas will be touched upon, with the emphasis on prevention, and additional resources will be given in the "Resources" section for those who wish a more in-depth discussion.

The information in this book is applicable to girls in high school, women embarking on a college/university experience, as well as mature women who are particularly vulnerable if they are re-entering the dating process after being in a long-term relationship. Not all men are rapists, and not all women are rape victims. Unfortunately, however, acquaintance rape can happen to women of all ages and socioeconomic backgrounds, regardless of their marital status or the length of time they've been in a relationship. (It is beyond the scope of this book to address rape within a marriage or rape in which the victim is male, however, the "Suggested Reading" section contains titles of reading material in those areas.)

Part of the difficulty in addressing the prevalence of date/acquaintance rape is that women tend not to be on their guard with men they know. There is a view of the rapist as a half-crazed maniac waiting in the bushes to pounce. Women in general take precautions against such an attacker, however statistics indicate that a woman is nearly five times more likely to be assaulted by someone she knows than by a stranger.

According to a study by the U.S. Department of Justice, 82 percent of the victims of rape or attempted rape knew or were acquainted with their attacker. Strangers accounted for only 18 percent of all rapes.[1] The issues of date and acquaintance rape first began to emerge from college and university campuses. Because of the prevalence of the problem for this age group, this book will focus frequently on prevention in the college or university setting. However, the tactics described are applicable to other settings and lifestyles as well.

Date/acquaintance rape prevention involves education, which must occur on two fronts simultaneously. Women need to learn the warning signs and how to extricate themselves from hazardous situations, and boys and men must learn new attitudes towards women, including that "No" is "No," and that silence is not consent.

It will take time and effort from parents and schools to change the way boys think about girls, and the way men think about women. Until that happens, girls and women will have to take a stronger stand for their rights to their own bodies. In truth, rape is a problem of male aggression and only men can change their attitudes, but at the point where the confrontation occurs, it becomes the woman's problem. Women must act as if their parents, brothers, friends, and even the police will probably not be there to protect them. The nation's law enforcement agencies are not responsible for preventing crime and protecting the citizens of the United States. Their primary purpose is to enforce the law, apprehend criminals, and investigate crime after it happens. Regardless, there is much a woman can do to take responsibility for her own safety.

Reality Check: Although many law enforcement agencies, both federal and local, have fine crime prevention departments, it is up to you to do all that you can to prevent crime and keep yourself from becoming a victim.

This book in many ways is actually about choices. The choices a woman makes at the beginning of a date and subsequent relationship give her the options she will have as the situation progresses and the relationship matures. The more options she has, the more power she has and the better her chances of getting out of a dangerous situation without being hurt.

It is important to understand that there is no one piece of advice that can be given to potential rape victims because each situation, each victim, and each perpetrator is different. If I were to tell a woman to physically resist with all her might by screaming, punching, and kicking, that advice would be ineffective if she tends to be passive and shy. She might not be able to bring herself to that action without getting hurt. If, however, she is very assertive and bold, it would be very difficult for her to be passive and non-confrontational in a struggle, even if that might be the best thing to do. It's also true that screaming might be a very effective response in a populated location, however it would be a waste of time and energy in an isolated environment. There is no right or wrong thing to do in all criminal confrontations. It depends on many factors.

How, then, does a woman know what is right or wrong, what will work and what will increase the violence? There are no guarantees. The best piece of advice I can give to girls and women is to take as many of the precautions outlined in this book as possible, and in all circumstances, listen to your inner guidance and trust your instincts.

Sometimes, even with her best efforts, a woman is unable to stop her attacker. For this reason, this book includes information on the best way to proceed after it is too late for prevention. A woman who knows what to do next and what to expect from the process has a better chance of finding the help she needs to recover fully and in a shorter time.

Reality Check: No matter what happens, rape is never the victim's fault.

This book is also about the choices a man makes in his relationships. Many men would never consider their own actions as rape, and yet they may press on even after a woman asks them to stop. Traditional attitudes hold a double standard that has some men seeing certain behaviors in women (such as how they dress, or their willingness to drink or take drugs), as a sign the woman is "asking for" sex. Men also may believe or assert that, once aroused, they are no longer in control of their sexual behavior. This is patently false. This book includes an "Advice for Men" chapter exploring these issues further.

Reality Check: At any age or any stage of arousal, a man is in complete control of his sexual behavior.

I hope this book will not just educate, but also will motivate all women, whatever their ages, to be more aware, awake, alert, and committed with all of their might to not becoming another victim.

This book will give you information about rape prevention, sexual harassment, stalking, and dating violence, but information without action will not make a difference in a woman's or man's life. I sincerely hope you will choose to take action before your choices are limited or taken away. There is no time to waste.

Take action now by learning how certain behaviors can help keep you safe.

Take action now by reporting a rape if you have been the victim of one.

Take action now by holding a workshop in your local bookstore or community center. Workshop kits based on this book are available. For more information, call (800) 727-8866, ext. 271.

This book is not likely to change anybody's attitude overnight about the opposite sex or his or her own gender. This only can be done through consistent education, but with the knowledge that this book has to offer, a young girl or woman might be able to recognize a dangerous man and/or situation before things get beyond her control.

This book also may be useful to men and boys and their fathers, who, consciously or unconsciously, have helped create an environment of rape and violence. In the final analysis, it is they who must stop the violence against women.

If even one rape is prevented as a result of this book, it will have served its purpose. However, it is my dream for the women of this nation that rape will disappear as an issue for them, and that men will understand that successful relationships are win/win, and that sex without consent is never an option.

section one

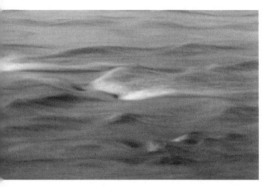

date/acquaintance rape prevention

chapter one

redefining rape

Rape is a sexual assault in which a person uses his penis or other object to commit vaginal, oral, or anal penetration of a victim, by force or threat of force, against the victim's will, or when the victim is physically and/or mentally unable to give consent.

Date rape is simply a rape that happens between two parties who are dating.

Acquaintance rape is a rape that happens when the victim and perpetrator are acquainted. The majority of rapes are actually acquaintance rapes, because in almost every case, the rapist gets to know the victim at least enough for her to drop her guard. Once she lets him into her confidence and begins to trust him, he strikes.

It is important to realize that not every victim of rape has signs of physical abuse. Just because her clothes are not shredded, or her bones aren't broken, doesn't mean she didn't resist or that she wasn't raped. The threat of force is, in many cases, just as intimidating as actual violence for the victim. The rapist has used fear to get control of her.

Even though rape is a life-threatening situation, the victim of acquaintance rape may not perceive it as such. The primary difference between stranger rape and date/acquaintance rape is the relationship between the victim and the rapist. The fact that she supposedly knows the rapist at least superficially, may make it more difficult to identify him as dangerous. This fact also may delude her friends and family into disbelieving her. Even more, knowing him can also dilute a woman's normal self-defense response to her attacker and cause her to hesitate in reporting the crime and seeking help for herself.

Date/acquaintance rape can happen to anyone who goes out on a date with or encounters a man who wants power over her in the form of sex and refuses to take no for an answer. Date/acquaintance rape accounts for 84 percent of all reported rapes[2], and yet it is estimated that only 5 percent of date/acquaintance rapes are reported.[3]

Is it possible that the most charming guy, who may be the leading quarterback for the high school football team, son of the mayor, president of the senior class, or the "perfect gentleman" who works or lives next door, can also be a rapist? Yes, if the circumstances are right and he thinks he can get away with it.

Reality Check: After you say, "No," it is rape.

Many men's definition of rape does not apply to their own behavior or that of their male friends. Many men, as well as many women, honestly believe that men cannot control themselves when they are sexually aroused. They believe the girl or woman is responsible both for arousing and for controlling the man. This is absolute rubbish. At any age, a man is perfectly able to control his sexual drive at any point, from first arousal to climax. However, the attitude that the man is not responsible for his actions with women is not a new idea. Many men, young and old, still have the fantasy that once aroused, they have a right to have sex with a woman, regardless of her wants, desires, or needs.

In a recent seminar at a prominent university fraternity in Georgia, I was amazed at the attitude of the men I was addressing. When asked, "How many 'No's' does it take before you finally stop your sexual pursuit?" the answer was, "Twenty or thirty." In fact, the president of the fraternity actually said, "If we give women the right to say 'No,' it gives them too much power." But, this kind of attitude is not exclusive to young college males. I was shocked when I gave a similar talk at a local church's non-denominational singles group. The participants were middle-aged, successful adults, including doctors, lawyers, and business executives. One actually stood up and said: "If a woman gets in my Mercedes without wearing a bra, she's asking for it!" Another man agreed, saying that any woman who goes up to a man's apartment, or allows a man into her apartment, is saying she wants to have sex. Such attitudes have been created by and taught by fathers, grandfathers, and yes, even mothers. Some women today still believe that it's a woman's job to control the man's behavior, and that women just have to tolerate the assaults.

Rape is about power. Men rape to get power over women. These men may feel powerless in their lives and so look for a way to increase their sense of self-worth by controlling and manipulating another "weaker" human being. Of course, this is a flawed idea, and rape doesn't give the rapist any lasting sense of power or self-worth, so he may continue to commit the crime until it becomes increasingly violent.

Reality Check: All rapists are serial rapists—they rape until they are stopped, averaging four to five rapes.[4] They rarely get help themselves, i.e., they don't stop until they're stopped.

Let's be clear about this point of control. A woman is not responsible for keeping a man in control of his own sexual responses. Each man is responsible for his own actions and no matter what a woman does, he has no right to any sexual contact with her against her will or without her knowledge. Rape is not just "he said/she said." Rape is not just a misunderstanding or the result of a lack of communication. Rape is an act of choice to commit a crime, to forcibly obtain power over another individual through the means of sexual assault.

Reality Check: Rape is not just a misunderstanding. Rape is a criminal act of choosing to overpower a woman and impose sexual intercourse on her without her consent or without her knowledge.

chapter two

what makes a woman vulnerable

The term "date/acquaintance rape" is used today to mean any situation in which the assailant merely is known to the victim. It should be understood that just because a woman is not dating the perpetrator doesn't mean he can't be a date/acquaintance rapist. Any man who has access to a woman can commit rape, including her doctor, lawyer, pastor, teacher, delivery man, salesman, brother, father, or friend.

Reality Check: You are five times more likely to be raped by someone you know than by a stranger.

All women, no matter their ages, should remember that being desperate for companionship or willing to settle for any relationship in order not to be alone could lead to dangerous situations. Younger women put themselves at risk because they may not realize the potential for danger. More mature women may derive a false sense of security from their past dating experience and feel they are "older and wiser."

Points of Vulnerability

A False Sense of Security

Date/acquaintance rape has touched nearly every college/university campus. Some educators, school officials, security staffs, and counselors are at a loss as to how to talk about stopping date rape without appearing to say that the university environment is unsafe. The reality is that a university is no more dangerous than any other high-density environment. However, many students approach this community environment with little or no awareness of the possible dangers.

First-year students are caught up with being on their own away from home. Tragically, the thrill of that freedom supersedes any thought that crime, specifically sexual assault, can happen to them. Most of the time, the excitement of having her own place as well as the determination to "make it" without parental controls can silence the real dangers of being a single woman on her own. The euphoria of living away from home on a college campus can create a false sense of security. For this reason, young women often get into situations, usually with alcohol and/or drugs, in which they are easy prey for more experienced men. It is common for students to take unnecessary risks while at school, because they feel invulnerable and protected in the college environment. In addition, young women may want to have a good time and party with alcohol just like the guys. This can be a dangerous mistake.

Mature women believe they can let their guard down because they have dated before. The dynamics of starting a new relationship can be very difficult, especially if the woman is dating again for the first time in many years. Beyond the ready-made social environment of a university campus, it can be more difficult to meet eligible men to date. Loneliness or insecurity may cause a woman to go out with men she might not ordinarily consider a good match, or she might meet men through personal ads or at singles bars where she really won't know anything about them before the dating begins. To some degree, a mature woman can use this to her advantage, as she is less likely to think she knows the man well after only a few encounters than a college student who may be fooled by the apparent safety of her campus environment. Although she's had more dating experience, a more mature woman may have forgotten the realities of being with a "stranger." Fears, insecurities, and family may complicate even the simplest of friendships. If she's going out with someone after a long marriage of twenty or thirty years, she may find out quickly that times have changed. She will need to think about her own physical safety and take the same precautions that a younger woman should take.

A False Sense of Intimacy

Thinking she knows a man after only one or two encounters, or after seeing him only in public, can place a woman in jeopardy. Familiarity breeds a dropping of one's guard. We are taught as youngsters to fear strangers, but not friends and acquaintances. Yet, we are in far greater danger from those we know (or think we know) than from a stranger. It is especially inconceivable to a young, naive woman that she could be assaulted by the very guy who shares her classes with her. Even a more mature woman, if she wants a relationship badly, will ignore her instincts and perhaps forgo cautionary behaviors in order to give herself a green light for the relationship. Remember, you never really can know an individual in one or two encounters. It is essential for women to observe a person in a variety of social situations over a period of time before allowing herself to be in a vulnerable situation with him.

Misleading Appearances

Appearances can be deceptive and are, unfortunately, not a foolproof indicator of what may be going on below the surface. The majority of rapists are middle-class white men. Neat clothing and grooming may be reassuring, but it is more to the point to inquire into a man's attitudes towards women and to carefully observe how he treats you.

The rapist desires power more than sex. We tend to think that men who are desirable and attractive can't be rapists. Not true. These kind of men can be just as mixed up about sexual coercion as less desirable men. The average rapist is not a twisted, ugly monster who lurks in the bushes. The average rapist looks like, and maybe is, the guy next door.

Drinking or Taking Drugs

The vast majority of date and acquaintance rapes involve abuse of alcohol and/or drugs. Chapter six will give you more information on this subject. However, it is a fact that alcohol affects women differently than men. This disparity is due mainly to three factors: body size, body composition, and levels of alcohol dehydrogenase enzyme. On average, women are smaller than men and carry more body fat, which contains little water to dilute alcohol in the bloodstream. In addition, women have less of the metabolizing enzyme alcohol dehydrogenase. Together, these differences between male and female physiology result in a higher concentration of alcohol in a woman's body than in a man's, for the same amount of alcohol ingested. A woman, generally speaking, will become more intoxicated on less alcohol than a man will.

Allowing Herself to Become Isolated

Criminals generally don't commit their crimes in view of the public. Likewise, a rapist will want to isolate his victim before he commits the crime. If a man attempts to sexually assault his date in a fairly public place, she stands a better chance of attracting attention and getting help than if she is alone with him. In order to prevent herself from becoming isolated, a woman must stay alert and plan ahead for how she would respond if the guy she is with shows signs of becoming dangerous. She must mentally prepare for that possibility.

Ignoring Warning Signals

What are the warning signals that a man sends when he intends to take advantage of a woman? There is more to this than just the "nagging feeling" that you have in the pit of your stomach that something is wrong. In his book, *The Gift of Fear,* Gavin de Becker, the world's foremost violence prevention specialist, outlines the behaviors criminals use on women. You should be careful if the man you are with does any of the following:

- Behaves as if the two of you are more intimate than you really are, or uses a lot of "we" phrases and appears to be working too hard to make you trust him.

- Appears to be trying to charm you, i.e., disorient you or allure you. "Niceness is a decision, a strategy of social intercourse. It is not a character trait. It has been said that men are nice when they pursue, women are nice when they reject," says de Becker. Behaving in a way that is unusual or excessively ingratiating can be a sign that a man is attempting to manipulate or control you.

- Gives too many details about himself. If he is giving you information that you are not asking for, and that most people would not volunteer, he may be lying to you.

- Makes slight criticisms and offers you the opportunity to prove him wrong. For example, if a man says: "You're so beautiful that you are probably stuck up and wouldn't go out with someone like me," he may be hoping you'll say to yourself, "I'm not a snob, and I'll prove him wrong by going out with him." This is manipulation, as the man may be trying to get you to think going out with him is your idea, and that you have something to prove to him.

- Spends lavishly on you and appears to be expecting something in return. If the man is attempting to make you feel that you owe him something, you may be in for trouble.

- Makes unsolicited promises, such as, "I'll just have one drink, and then I'll go." An unsolicited promise can be a way to buy time or to give the man an opportunity to get control over you or the situation. If you have made it clear that you want your date to leave, and he says he'll leave "just as soon as I have another drink," or, "after I use the bathroom," or, "after I make a phone call," etc., you will have to be firm and communicate clearly and strongly your desire to leave or for him to leave.

- Attempts to control you. If your date is not allowing you to participate in decisions about the date, if he insists on ordering for you in a restaurant, on "taking care of everything," or suggests that you don't trust him, these may be warning signals.

- Says derogatory things about women. Expressing an attitude that women are inferior to men, that women should obey men, or that women are responsible for a man's sexual response can all be signs of trouble.

- Doesn't accept "No" for an answer. If he offers you a drink, or suggests that you go somewhere with him, and continues to press you even after you say, "No" you will have to be very firm and communicate very clearly. If he won't accept "No," for an answer on something small, he may not in regard to sex, either.

Ignoring Her Inner Guidance

We live in a male-dominated culture that often debunks intuition and inner guidance. Women who trust their inner guidance may be ridiculed by men for not being logical and realistic. The truth is that your inner guidance or intuition is the most trustworthy and dependable barometer. The above manipulations and tactics that most criminals use also can be used by perfectly harmless men. So the problem is, how does a woman know when one or more of these techniques is being used by a man with dangerous intentions? The answer lies in her intuition. When it comes to danger, intuition is always right in at least two important ways: (I) It is responding to something real. (2) It has your best interests at heart.

The following levels of intuition will give you an idea of how intuition works. According to de Becker, your intuition builds from curiosity to hunches, to gut feelings, to doubt, to hesitation, to suspicion, to apprehension, and finally to fear. Fear is the most important and critical. If you feel fear in a situation, honor it.

The question then arises, "What makes a woman *invulnerable?*" It is not so much a question of invulnerability, since all of us are vulnerable to crime. It is rather a question of what makes a woman stronger and less likely to become a victim? The answer is knowledge, combined with a determination to act in her own best interest, regardless of what others think or do. The following chapters will give you that knowledge. The determination to use it is up to you.

chapter three

one woman's story

Date rape generally does not happen out of the blue. In most cases, there are warning signals and a progression of events that, if understood, shed some light on how the rapist operates and how the intended victim may have played right into his hands.

The following story of one survivor is symptomatic of many of the things that can happen to a woman when her date/acquaintance refuses to honor her wishes and decides to take from her what she does not want to share. The story is divided into ten stages that will serve to illustrate how this particular date rape progressed from innocent first contact to assault and finally to rape. The names of Helen and Jim are aliases to protect the real persons involved. Helen's story is only one example, but it contains many of the elements that recur frequently in incidents of date/acquaintance rape.

"I guess my story is not that unusual—many of my friends in college were also raped. We all suffered and we continue to be traumatized by what happened to us during that time. I've since learned that rape victims like me take longer to heal because we've had our trust taken from us. It's difficult for me to trust men. I'm always thinking: What does he have on his mind? Will he rape me when my guard is down?"

Stage 1: Introduction and background. At this point, he may seem to be the perfect gentleman.

"Jim and I met during college. He was running for student body president, and I was one of the people in his campaign. He was enormously popular, and I guess I was as impressed as every other girl who was with him. I worked really hard to get him elected and after the election, he asked me out. We went to lunch."

Comment: In this first stage, Jim appeared the ideal man— successful, bright, an honor student, and tremendously popular.

Prevention: Helen thought she knew him, but she only knew the "public" side of Jim. It is important to remember that even though you may have spent time with him in class, at a party, at the office, or in a social situation, this doesn't mean you know all about him. He may be showing you only one side of his personality.

Jim and all men need to understand that what works in the business and sports arena doesn't work in relationships. There is a tendency to believe that persistence and drive are the building blocks of success, that the world is a win/lose world, in which the end justifies the means. In relationships, a win/lose belief system is totally inappropriate and destructive.

Stage 2: His comments and attitudes about women surface. It may become obvious at this point that he does not really respect women.

"I didn't really hear some of the things that he said until I thought about them afterwards. He made several remarks about women and how they tease men to get what they want and then complain when they get 'it.' I don't know why it didn't ring a bell in my head, but I guess I wasn't as much into the women's movement as I am today, so I let it pass."

Comment: Many women are still in the habit of tolerating men's insensitive remarks and ignoring their behavior. They often will make excuses for men and will not confront such negative attitudes, even if the attitude is abusive. In this situation, Jim's comment seems to indicate that he sees women and men in an adversarial context, i.e., "them and us."

Many men will reveal their true feelings and attitudes about women through their off-hand comments when their guard is down. They may say disparaging things about women and their bodies. Jim made an important statement about women teasing men with their bodies and then complaining when the man gets turned on. Jim is making the common statement that many men with traditional attitudes make, that a woman is responsible for the behavior of a man. **This is a warning signal!**

He also is saying that a man will do what he wants and is justified, especially if he feels that the woman has led him on to the point of no return. Jim is making the common statement that once a man gets turned on, he can't control himself.

Reality Check: No one turns anyone else on. We turn ourselves on.

When Jim or anyone else sees someone and feels sexually aroused, they have used their mind and their thoughts to excite themselves about the person at whom they're looking. It is also true that if you turn yourself on, you can turn yourself off. Jim is totally in control of his thoughts, feelings, and emotions. Helen has no part in the way his mind or body operates.

Prevention: Helen might have corrected him, and stated that a man is responsible for his own behavior, regardless of a woman's actions. This would have communicated to Jim that Helen is not like some of the more passive women he may have dated. At this point, Jim might have made the decision that Helen would not be an easy target and changed his mind about the assault. Statements like Jim's may indicate that the man may feel disconnected from women and as though he has to make his personality and power felt. These feelings are often expressed unconsciously in the course of a man's conversation, especially when he is relaxed and speaking in an unfiltered manner.

Stage 3: He treats you as if you are less than his equal. He makes decisions for you and is obsessed with control.

"A couple of days later, we met for drinks in a restaurant/bar off campus. He immediately took charge of me and the whole evening. He insisted on ordering dinner for me. I was impressed with his sophistication and how the waiters catered to his commands. No wonder he was class president, he seemed born to command. He started instructing me on exactly how to eat my dinner, saying he was tired of girls who didn't know proper etiquette. I was torn between feeling pampered by his attentions and yet feeling at the same time totally ignorant, as if I had no opinion or knowledge about how to act. I realize now how all of this was only a means to control and intimidate me."

Comment: Remember that control is the issue here. Jim is testing the waters to see how Helen will respond. His "take charge" attitude may appear to be flattering to some women who want to be taken care of, but it is a danger signal that he wants to control you and your behavior. Often, a man with traditional attitudes seems to need to control a woman and will go to almost any means to subdue her and/or convince his peers that the woman is under his control. He may equate his ability to subjugate women with feeling in control of his own life. In a marriage, this kind of man may insist on control of the bank account and finances as well as on making all of the major decisions. He may also deny his wife, whom he believes to be his property, the opportunity to work, go to school, or even have friends. He may be extremely jealous and publicly humiliate her in front of their friends. This kind of control often escalates into domestic violence.

Prevention: In retrospect, Helen saw Jim's behavior at this stage as controlling. If she had felt uncomfortable at the time, Helen could have insisted on ordering for herself. This might have communicated again to Jim that she's a woman with a mind of her own who cannot be controlled.

Remember, if you find yourself in this type of situation, you need to stay alert to your comfort level with his behavior. Keep in mind that accumulating controlling behaviors may be a warning signal. Continually gauge your own comfort level and inner guidance.

Stage 4: He plies you with alcohol and drugs—the assault begins! This is his attempt to reduce your ability to resist.

"We drank for a while, and I wasn't intending to drink too much, but he kept ordering for me and insisting that I drink up. At first I thought, 'Why not?' I didn't mind having a good time and anyway, I trusted him. God, you know, he was student body president, and every girl in the place was kind of admiring me for who I was out with. I definitely remember thinking, 'Why is he doing this? Why does he want me to drink so much?' I wasn't really sure what was going on during all this, but back then, everyone in our class got drunk at least once a week anyhow, so it was probably no big deal. I don't know what happened to me after that. I think I blacked out. I was really drunk."

Comment: Alcohol is a great enabler of violent behavior. It tends to break down the inhibitions in both men and women. In many cases, getting drunk is a prelude to being unable to stop an assault that may come later. In some cases, the perpetrator will not drink as much as his intended victim. This is because he knows that too much alcohol inhibits sexual performance.

Jim was very obvious in his desire for Helen not only to drink, but to become intoxicated. Many men still think that the reason a woman drinks is to "loosen up." He feels he needs an advantage and alcohol is his advantage. Helen makes the statement that everyone in her class got drunk at least once a week. The most common reason for drinking in college is not to loosen up, but to get drunk.

Prevention: Drinking and drugs play an important part in the commission of date rape because if you drink or take drugs, you run the risk of numbing your senses and making yourself confused. Alcohol reduced Helen's chances to prevent the crime. The more she drinks, the less control she has. Often, by the time a woman realizes what has happened, it is too late to take significant preventative action. Stay alert and aware of what's happening around you and in your own mind. It is important to recognize what your alcohol limit is and to know the possibilities for danger when you go beyond that limit. Helen could have refused to go beyond her own limit. She could have ordered for herself, insisting that she not drink to excess or just not drink at all.

Reality Check: Alcohol has been shown to be a significant factor in the vast majority of date and acquaintance rapes, and in over 90 percent of all campus crime.

What a man needs to understand is that if he is successful in getting the woman drunk, he puts himself in jeopardy with the law, because if the woman is incapable of saying no, getting away, or even resisting his advances, then he is, by law, committing rape.

If you don't drink liquor or take drugs at all, you are less likely to be incapacitated and confused during a date/acquaintance rape situation.

Stage 5: He manipulates you into an isolated area. Now you are alone. The security you may be depending upon (a party/gathering of friends) no longer is there.

"The next thing I remember, I was in his truck and he was taking me to his place. He kept saying not to worry because there would be a lot of people there, a party of some kind, and anyway he said he'd take care of me. I didn't know at the time what he really meant. But I would soon find out. I wasn't feeling too hot at the time. Drinking too much gives me a headache. I told him that I might throw up. He said I'd better not; it was a brand new truck. It didn't matter to him, he just kept driving. When we got there, I didn't see any other cars and that's the first time that voice inside me said, 'Get out,' but I was so drunk that I couldn't think straight. God, I should have listened to that voice. He said that maybe the people had parked somewhere else, and were probably waiting for us. Somehow I knew he was lying."

Comment: Criminals depend upon isolation to commit their crimes. Yes, this is a crime about to happen and he is a criminal when he commits it. It is imperative that you not become isolated and alone with him unless you absolutely trust him. Jim did what many men do when they are planning to rape. They must have unlimited access to the intended victim without interference. Criminals use various means to trick their unsuspecting victims into positions of vulnerability. Helen thought she would be safe because she was supposedly going to a party with lots of other people. She was tricked.

Prevention: At this stage, a woman needs to be alert for inconsistencies that could lead to isolation. If there was a party that Jim wanted to attend, why didn't he mention it earlier at the start of the evening? Helen could have questioned him about the party.

Once you're in his car, your options are limited. It's always a good idea to take your own car and meet him wherever you are going. This way you have a way home. Had she not been drinking, Helen could have insisted on taking her own vehicle.

In most traumatic situations, especially crimes, potential victims recall having sensed some kind of warning signal. (This warning signal may be an inner voice, a vision, or just a feeling of dread or impending doom.) How important is that voice/feeling? It is absolutely imperative that you listen to it and take action, heeding the warning that your intuition is giving you. As soon as Helen sensed that Jim was lying to her, she could have insisted on going home.

Stage 6: Confusion and limited escape.

"Why did I go in? When we got upstairs, of course there was no one there, I knew it! He was all over me from the moment we got inside the door. He said, 'You've been teasing me all evening.' He started ripping my clothes, saying, 'I gotta have it, I gotta have it,' like 'it' was something not connected to me, a thing that wasn't human. I tried to talk to him. I said, 'No, not this way, I don't want to.' He wasn't listening to me! I just couldn't believe this was happening to me. He was so popular. He was an honor student. He was student body president. I said, 'This can't happen to me. Stop it, please! Let me go! I want to go home.' I told him if he didn't let me go, I would be sick. He laughed and slapped me. He said that if I made a mess, I'd have to clean it up.

"When he slapped me, I knew I was in big trouble. I tried to get away from him, but I didn't know where I was. I realized I had left my purse in his truck and I certainly couldn't ask him for a ride home now. I kept thinking about how I was trapped there with him with no way home."

Comment: Confusion has led to denial that the situation is happening to her. In many cases of date rape, precious seconds and minutes are lost while the intended victim is going through denial. Over and over, she may question herself and the choices she made that evening that have brought her to that point. This process comes from our unending need to understand what is happening to us. We keep saying: "Why is this happening? What did I do wrong? Why did I go out with him? Why didn't I listen to my guidance?" and finally, "Why is he doing this?"

You do not have the luxury at this moment to try and figure out why all this is happening. There are no simple answers anyway. Now is the time to act and act quickly.

Reality Check: It is important to understand no matter what choices you make in a dating situation, you did not choose to be raped. The rapist has taken that choice away from you. He is the one who has chosen to commit a violent crime.

The alcohol added to Helen's confusion at this point as well as her inability to believe what was happening to her. She had trusted Jim. He was the opposite of a stereotypical rapist in every sense of the word. All the reasons why he couldn't be the kind of person to rape flashed through her mind—honor student, student body president, and, of course, popularity. After all, if the other students liked him so much then he can't be doing this, right? Wrong! This confusion also is common with older, more established men. If a man is successful in business can he be a rapist? Yes. If a man is rich and has prestige, can he be a rapist? Yes. If a man is in a position of trust and moral authority (like a doctor, lawyer, or minister) can he be a rapist? Yes.

Helen was in a state of denial at this point, which didn't change until Jim slapped her. Once he slapped her, the reality of her situation came crashing in on her. Even though she tried to get away, it was too late. Her options were limited. As in most crimes, the best time to escape is within the first few moments of a confrontation. The longer you wait, the less control you are apt to have. It is within these first few seconds or minutes that the criminal probably is not yet in total control, so your options for escape are fairly good if you can stop thinking and start acting.

Prevention: There aren't many options open to Helen at this point. The question is how can a woman cope with the mounting confusion she might experience in a situation like this, and most importantly, prevent the confusion from overtaking her.

First of all, breathe! Fear tends to stop your breathing and this causes less oxygen to get to your brain, which contributes to the confusion. Confusion also stems from being unable to make decisions. You must, at this very critical moment, empty your mind of all the "what-ifs." Your only task is to escape. You don't have time to mull over all of the choices you made or the "Why is this happening to me?" questions. Tell your mind to stop thinking about that and concentrate on survival.

The most common reason people fail to use weapons or martial arts training for self-defense is that they keep analyzing the risks versus the benefits. They think and think and think, until they have lost control of the situation. You must simplify your thinking and your actions in a situation like this, shutting down your analytical thoughts. Your life is on the line; you must act decisively with 100 percent commitment to your own well-being.

Stage 7: He threatens you with physical violence or verbally abuses you to get you to cooperate.

"I just didn't know what to do. I screamed at him that he had no right to do this. He said: 'You're all alike, all of you! You lead a man on, and then this happens. You complain and scream bloody murder that it's not what you want. It's what you wanted all along! I saw you looking at me when I was giving all those speeches. You're just playing hard to get. Well go ahead and play hard to get, cause now it's hard, and you're gonna get it!'"

Comment: Jim's words begin to express hatred and pent-up frustration at women. There are a number of cases where a man committed rape when a "triggering event" happened. This triggering event may be an incident that reminds the man of past troubles with a woman. In this kind of rape, the current rape victim represents someone else, or all women in general. Jim may have been taking out years of misunderstandings and hurt feelings on Helen. He may even have been, in his mind, raping someone else. The point is, there is no way for a woman to know she is triggering this kind of response. It has nothing to do with her, therefore she can in no way be considered responsible for the man's behavior.

Most reported date rapes are committed with minimal to moderate acts of violence. The rapist generally depends on his physical size and weight to control his victim, without resorting to the additional brutality that in the majority of cases accompanies stranger-to-stranger rape.

Jim actually had already used mild violence on Helen and had made it clear that he would do whatever was necessary to get what he wanted. He justified what he did and what he intended to do. For many women, the threat of violence is so shocking, coming from this guy whom they trusted, they freeze and can't defend themselves. Whether the man uses physical violence, emotional force, or intimidation on a woman, it still steals her ability to choose.

Reality Check: The threat of violence is just as intimidating and paralyzing as violence itself! A woman being raped overwhelmingly

and accurately believes that her life is in danger. For this reason, Dr. Peg Ziegler, former director of the Atlanta, Georgia, Rape Crisis Center, has called the crime of rape the "unfinished murder."

Prevention: At this point, Helen may have been able to turn the tables on Jim if she had pulled out all the stops and physically fought him rather than submit. Fighting back against a date rapist is a viable alternative, however, many women do not believe that a rape is happening until it's over.

Stage 8: The actual assault or rape. After the assault, he may minimize his actions or question the importance you have placed on the assault, i.e., he acts as if nothing has happened.

"After he raped me, he acted like it was my fault. He said, 'You know, you really shouldn't turn a guy on like that. You could get hurt.' I couldn't believe what he was saying. It was like he became this father-figure, all protective and concerned about my welfare. He kept talking to me, trying to make conversation. It was like nothing happened. He actually helped me get dressed. I was so torn up inside that I was shaking. I couldn't keep from crying. He drove me home, all the way talking about me being careful and not to trust strangers around here, because it wasn't safe. I didn't say anything. I was still in shock. I went up to my room and just sat there holding myself. I remember rocking back and forth, like when I was little. He called me later that night and said that maybe we should go out next week. He actually thanked me for a wonderful night and said he'd see me tomorrow in biology class."

Comment: Jim did what many date rapists do after the assault: he behaved in a conciliatory manner towards his victim. He helped Helen get dressed, acted concerned about her safety, and drove her home. He called her later that night to thank her. This may seem like two separate men. But it only serves to point out the dichotomy of beliefs that some men have about women and about their own sexual behavior. It is apparent that Jim does not understand that he has committed rape.

Jim's behavior is consistent with what the FBI calls "The Gentleman Rapist" or "Power Reassurance Rapist." Though he is certainly no gentleman, the FBI uses the term because this rapist tends to use low levels of force and to rely on threats of violence. He fantasizes that he and the woman are just having sex, and that is why he may later thank her for a "wonderful night." He pursues the relationship, apparently not comprehending that he has committed a crime. If the woman charges him with rape, he will be totally confused and in a high state of denial.

Prevention: It is important to understand that the ultimate source of rape prevention is with the man. Jim's determination to get control, his need to feel power, his lack of understanding and compassion for Helen, and his disregard for the law and what is right are what needs to be addressed. Attempts at analysis and understanding of Jim's behavior are, in reality, a waste of time, especially for Helen. For her, it doesn't matter what or who drove him to commit rape.

Reality Check: At some level, the rapist made a choice to commit a violent crime and probably thought he could get away with it.

Helen could have emphatically told Jim what he was about to do or had done and her intentions to report the crime to the police or to campus security. However, she may not have wanted to aggravate him before or after the rape by telling him she planned to report it. If the full impact of what he had done had occurred to him, he might have stopped himself, however there is also a chance a rapist will resort to physical violence to ensure a woman's silence. Although it is now too late for prevention in this instance, reporting the incident can possibly contribute to stopping future rapes by this man.

Stage 9: After the assault, the symptoms may continue for many years. The most important bond—trust—has been broken. Self-criticism, guilt, and self-hatred may follow as the victim tries to understand what happened, and why.

"I didn't go to biology class the next day. I left school and went home to my parents, but I couldn't tell them. I knew they wouldn't understand. My parents are good Catholics; they hardly even drink. I just couldn't take their guilt. I had enough of my own. I left school. I just couldn't go back. He was so popular, so respected by everybody, that I just thought no one would ever believe me. You know today, ten years later, I still haven't told my parents. Maybe if it happened today, I wouldn't leave school because there's more awareness about date rape. Now it seems like everyone's talking about it. I'm glad. Several years later, I talked with some of the girls with whom I went to school and they told me he had raped several girls and no one ever reported it. I think the guy's an attorney today."

Comment: One of the most common consequences of a date/acquaintance rape is the perpetrator continues his life unaffected—at least on the surface—while the survivor is barely able to put the pieces of her life back together. Her life is ruined and his is unmarked. It is for this reason that women should think very carefully about reporting the crime. In many cases, a woman will be able to recover faster if she has acknowledged the incident, filed a police report, and pressed charges. If she can do this, difficult as it is, she may feel less guilty about the situation and honestly feel that there's only one criminal person at fault, and it's not her. Of course, in order to facilitate the healing process, she must get help and support from therapists and other support groups. This will let her know that she is not alone and that there are people who care.

For Helen, as for many women, the trauma lasted for years. She quit school and, even to this day, is affected in her relationships with men, though it has been many years. Some psychologists have said that the trauma and broken trust after a date/acquaintance rape lingers for many years. A woman raped by a stranger may not have to deal with the trust issue to the same degree. A woman raped by someone she knows and trusts is in a doubly difficult situation. She also may not be believed by friends, relatives, and authorities. Not being believed may add to her feelings of betrayal, worthlessness, guilt, and loneliness. It may cause her to bury her feelings altogether and pretend the crime never happened, which can cause severe long-term damage both emotionally and physically.

Reality Check: You can heal and you can recover after a rape, but only if you survive the assault.

Hindsight is always 20/20, and it is vital for the survivor of rape to understand that there are no right or wrong choices. If you are attacked and survive, then you did the right thing, no matter what you did. Your top priority in the attack is to survive. Stop the rape if you can; if you can't, then your next goal is to survive and to heal.

There is help for women who have been raped. Support groups have sprung up all over the country to help women deal with this trauma and to recover their feelings of self-worth. There are thousands of Internet sites available for you to get connected with people and organizations who care. If you don't have a computer, go to a friend who has Internet access or use the computer at your local library. There are many caring and qualified therapists and support groups that can help in the healing process.

Don't try to deal with it alone. Get help from people who will believe you and not judge you. You are not alone!

chapter four

the date rape triangle

Regardless of where it takes place, the crime of date/acquaintance rape involves three factors, which I call "The Date Rape Triangle." These three factors are:

Criminal Intent—more than half of all rapes are clearly planned.[5]

Alcohol/Drugs—on many occasions, the woman becomes physically immobilized to the degree that she has consumed alcohol and/or drugs.

Isolation—the criminal generally must get his victim to a place where there are no witnesses.

Diagram I: The Date Rape Triangle

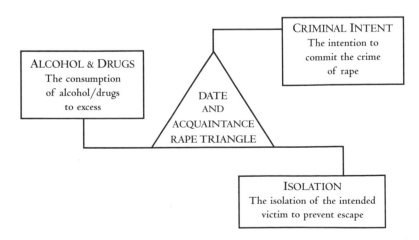

29

Once these three factors come together, escape is limited and a date/acquaintance rape is a possibility.

**Reality Check: Rape can happen to anyone,
regardless of her behavior and circumstances.**

In most cases, however, the potential victim of date/acquaintance rape has the ability to control two out of three of the date rape triangle factors. She can control how much alcohol and/or drugs she consumes, and whether she becomes isolated and alone with the rapist. If she can break just one side of the Date Rape Triangle, she will greatly reduce her chances of becoming a victim, but remember there are no guarantees.

Planning Ahead

Crime victims who fare the worst in a confrontation with a criminal generally have one thing in common. They thought it would never happen to them, and took no precautions or even gave any thought to protecting themselves.

It may help you in the long run to put yourself hypothetically in the position of being attacked, asking yourself, "If he did this, what would I do?" It's a way of rehearsing the situation before it ever occurs, so you can make some plans or preparations. You might give some thought to this for a few minutes while you prepare for a date. It seems unappealing, but it can make all the difference if the worst should come to pass.

Questions to Ask Yourself

What if you see signs that a location or party is high risk for women? What would you do?
What if your date is not all he said he was? What would you do?
What if he tried to rape you? What would you do?
What if you could not get home? What would you do?

What if you could not fight back because you were drunk?

What would you do? Could you get away?

If you did get away, where would you go?

How would you get help?

Who could you call in an emergency?

Take the time and write down some answers to these hypothetical questions, and what you might do to change the outcome. The more you have considered what might happen in various situations and how you would respond, the better prepared you are.

Fifteen Ways to Prevent Date and Acquaintance Rape

1. Communicate up front with him. If you want a platonic relationship, say so. If there is to be no sex, say so.

2. Be assertive with him about sex; he can't read your mind.

3. Make sure that your body language matches your words.

4. Wear clothes and shoes that allow for a full range of movement and in which you can move quickly if you must.

5. Introduce him to your roommate, friends, or family before you go out, and tell them when you will return.

6. If this is your first date with him, meet him during daylight hours and take your own car.

7. Remember, isolated spots can be dangerous. Meet him in public and stay around other people.

8. Fraternity Rush parties and all parties where there is excessive alcohol consumption can be dangerous. Do not go to isolated bedrooms or basements, and do not allow yourself to be alone with men with no other female present.

9. Alcohol and drugs are tools of date rapists. Getting high or drunk will make his job easier and your escape more difficult.

10. Always pour your own drinks, even if you are drinking only soft

drinks. Never let someone else carry or watch your drink for you. If you have any reason to suspect that your drink has been spiked, throw it away and remove yourself from the situation.

11. Always carry a telephone calling card, or better yet a cellular phone, and enough cash to get help and get home. If you need to make a call for help and it is at all possible, excuse yourself and go to the women's bathroom or some other safe place to make your call. Do not do it where he can hear your conversation.

12. Never leave a bar or party with a man you do not know or are not absolutely sure about.

13. Take a self-defense course in order to raise your self-confidence and learn many precautions that you can take that are suited to your individual personality. (Note that in order to actually be able to successfully defeat an attacker in a confrontation, you will probably need more than one lesson.)

14. Be aware of what is happening around you, and trust your instincts. Do not let a man intimidate you or make you feel uncomfortable. If your inner guidance tells you to leave, do so at once.

15. Have a plan in your mind that you can follow if your date gets abusive or dangerous. Remember that your best chance to escape is at the beginning of the confrontation. Don't delay or second guess yourself. Commit to your own safety and do whatever you have to do to escape. Don't worry about what other people may think about you if you feel you are in danger. Act and act quickly.

chapter five

danger spots

Helen's story illustrates many of the most common elements of date rape, but remember that date and acquaintance rape can happen anywhere and any time of day or night. In most cases of rape, the intended victim let down her guard for a moment or longer, which gave the rapist enough time to get control of the situation and prevent her escape. This can happen in a parking lot, a hallway, on the street, in a car, or in a home. There are three danger spots that women should be particularly aware of: bars, fraternity houses, and college athletic parties.

Bars

Meeting men in bars is obviously hazardous for any woman. Many men go to bars primarily to meet women, and the women they meet there are, *in their opinion,* available. Alcohol and bars attract what some men call "bad" girls and "loose" women. The mere fact that you are there presupposes, *in their minds,* that you are asking for sex. In addition, in the majority of date/acquaintance rapes, alcohol and drugs play a part in breaking down the resistance of the woman, as well as releasing the male's inhibitions. Be extra cautious with any man you meet in a bar.

Fraternity Houses

Fraternity houses can be a particular danger spot for college-aged women. A fraternity house can be a breeding ground of hyped-up masculinity and machismo. There is a strong sense of bonding and competition among the guys that may result in unexpectedly aggressive behavior. A first-year female student is usually more vulnerable because she does not know the facts about campus life and also may not be familiar with hot spots on campus or the reputations of some men who, if given the chance, will take advantage of her. She is also vulnerable because she has just left home, wants to make a good impression with the most popular guys on campus, and may drink to excess just to go along and be accepted.

Reality Check: The most dangerous time for a woman in her first year of college occurs from move-in day to the first holiday break. This is when most Rush parties happen.

Rush Week is a time of much excitement on campus. The fraternities are busily involved in getting new members and there are usually a great number of parties. Unfortunately, where there are parties there may be alcohol and drugs. Some fraternities have what they call "Little Sisters," although some Greek fraternities and college administrations have now outlawed them and most fraternities have discontinued this practice. Little Sisters are generally first-year female students who help the fraternities during Rush Week. These Little Sisters often become Little Victims because they end up the prime targets for acquaintance and gang rape.

A recent study in *Gender* magazine distinguished two types of fraternity houses: high-risk and low-risk. Most women surveyed identified some fraternities as having more sexually aggressive members and a higher probability for rape. These same women considered other fraternity houses as "safe" houses or low-risk, where a woman could go to party and feel secure that she would not be in danger.

High-Risk Fraternity Houses

Without going into a great deal of psychological analysis of why some fraternity houses are more dangerous than others, here are some things to watch out for.

Uneven gender ratios at parties: Some parties have more men than women, others have more women than men.

Gender segregation: Men and women in different groups. Many men often at a bar area drinking together.

Men treat women disrespectfully: They will often engage in jokes, conversations, and behaviors that degrade women, i.e., rating women's bodies from 1 to 10, or with thumbs up or thumbs down.

Bathrooms are filthy: The toilets often will be clogged, with vomit in the sink.

The atmosphere is less friendly: Men and women rarely smile or laugh. Men are openly hostile and threatening. There may be profanity, touching, pushing, or name calling by men and women.

Gender self-consciousness: Students at high-risk parties seem self-conscious about women being there and there is awareness that the atmosphere is sexually charged.

Dancing changes around midnight: Dancing early in the evening is often just between women and around midnight couples start dancing erotically.

Propositions for isolation begin: The men will try to pick up the women and use some excuse to get them isolated.

Breakfast bragging: The day after a party at a high risk house often will start with the brothers bragging about how many women they had sex with.

Low-Risk Fraternity Houses

Although these houses are, according to the survey, less risky, that should not give women a false sense of safety and license to drop their guard. You still need to watch the alcohol consumption, guard your drink so that it cannot be tampered with, and be careful of isolation. In general, low-risk fraternities were more likely to exhibit the following characteristics:

Equal number of women and men at parties.

Social atmosphere is friendly with interaction between women and men.

Men and women dance in groups and together.

Many couples are in relationships and display affection.

Friendly conversation within coed groups.

Appearances that many people know each other.

When pushing occurs, participants tend to apologize.

Bathrooms are usable and well supplied.

It is apparent that the differences between high-risk fraternity houses and low-risk houses can give a woman signals about the kind of behavior that is likely to occur during a party. If you find yourself at a high-risk fraternity party, it might be wise to find a way to leave as soon as possible before something happens.

Progress at Fraternities

The alcohol-soaked fraternity culture is beginning to change. As legal liability and bad publicity soar in the wake of high-profile rapes and alcohol-related hazing deaths, fraternities are taking action. Nine national fraternities say local chapters will be required to go "dry" within a few years. Across the nation, about 40 percent of colleges have established "relationship agreements" with their fraternities specifying higher expectations and responsibilities. According to Jonathan Brant, Executive Vice President of the National Interfraternity Conference in Indianapolis, Indiana, which represents sixty-six men's fraternities nationwide, "There is a genuine desire among fraternity leaders to change the culture, particularly in chapters focused on hedonism and alcohol."

The University of Delaware has done just that after disgust over hazing and drinking violations nearly drove the Faculty Senate to ban Greek Rush in 1992. Instead, the school created the Five-Star Program, which grades fraternities and sororities annually in five audited areas: academics, financial management, university and community service, campus involvement, and new-member education. Delaware's plan is working. Today, three fraternities of the nineteen on campus have five stars, seven have three- and four-star rankings, and two are two-star fraternities. For the first time in a decade, fraternities achieved a collective grade point average higher than the overall men's average on campus. Where once fraternities had open kegs at rush parties, "Dry Rush" is now the norm at Delaware and at many other universities.

College Sports Celebrations

Whereas fraternities have had to make changes in their behaviors or face the possibility that the university would close chapters or ban them altogether, athletic groups and events, which can be even more dangerous, have in most cases avoided change. The reason lies in the prestige that a winning football or basketball team brings to the university and the alumnae dollars that go along with a championship season.

Male athletes can be particularly dangerous if given the right situation and sufficient alcohol to loosen inhibitions. Some athletes view relationships like opponents on the field, as adversaries. They have a high status on campus and are trained and rewarded for aggression. The male bonding that is natural in team sports, also can contribute to gang rape. Athletes may be protected by their coaches and the university, and kept from facing the consequences of actions such as drunkenness or assault if they are valuable to the team.

Danger Spot Prevention

Many of the precautions that apply to date rape also apply to social situations that may end up being danger spots.

Consider that the same warning signs in terms of male behavior exist in high-risk bars, fraternity parties, and sports or athletic celebrations. Once again, do not allow yourself to become isolated with one man or with a group of men. Generally, women, especially younger ones, tend to think that they're safer if they are in a group. This is true only if there are other females in the group.

Since alcohol and drugs are rape enablers, you should be very cautious about your consumption, especially if you notice any of the high-risk signs.

Remember that a drug can be slipped into your drink when you are not looking. Do not let your drink out of your sight or control, and do not drink it if you have any doubts whatsoever.

Keep your wits about you. Be aware of what is happening, and be prepared to escape and get to safety if your inner guidance tells you to do so.

chapter six

alcohol and drugs: the rape enablers

Many people still believe that alcohol and drugs can make for great times both on and off campus. However, there are inherent dangers that come not only from accidents and overdoses but also from changes in behavior that contribute to rape.

It is important to understand what happens to people when they drink and take drugs. It is also important to see and understand the relationship of alcohol and drugs to date rape.

Reality Check: Alcohol is not an aphrodisiac. Alcohol is a depressant. Too much alcohol inhibits male sexual performance and a woman's ability to fight back.

About 75 percent of the men and more than half of the women involved in date/acquaintance rapes had been drinking or taking drugs before the attack.[6] In addition, alcohol is a contributing factor in the vast majority of campus crimes, thus it is doubly important for universities to take action to curb excessive alcohol consumption on campus and at school-sponsored activities. According to a nationwide scientific study, approximately 86 percent of all college students drink,[7] and the main reason given for drinking by college students was to get drunk.[8]

From what I have learned from those who attend my seminars, many men are sexually inhibited, and alcohol has gained a reputation as a sexual stimulant simply by contributing to the loss of inhibitors. However, large amounts of alcohol can have disastrous effects on sexual performance. This is why a man who is planning a date rape later in the evening will ply his date with lots of alcohol, constantly refilling her glass, but will not drink so much that he becomes drunk himself.

The Effects of Alcohol

In addition to its physiological effects, alcohol also has a tendency to release inhibitions and make it easier to break customs or inner codes of behavior, leading to actions people would never take while sober. In other words, alcohol may tend to shut down the conscience in some people and give courage to others. Psychological research indicates that we all have a "wall" or "barrier"—a code of ethics and morality—that we won't cross. Alcohol seems to confuse the line, allowing an individual to do things he/she would never normally do. Alcohol can and does affect some men's perception of women. This can lead to violence in some individuals.

Alcohol complicates the situation for a number of reasons. Firstly, men who hold traditional, double-standard attitudes may believe that a woman who is willing to drink or take drugs with them can't be a "good girl," and must be the kind of person who also will go along with sex. A woman's willingness to drink or take drugs *in and of itself* may cause the man to believe the woman is "asking for it." He may believe that this places the responsibility for the rape on the woman and not on himself. (This double standard never faults men who drink, take drugs, and sleep around.)

Secondly, alcohol or drug consumption will cause a woman's senses to become dulled and clouded. In a sexual assault, she is going to need all of her wits about her to be able to get out of the situation. Many times, a woman is too intoxicated to understand where the rapist is taking her or even what he's going to do until it's too late and the assault has begun. Once the assault has reached the advanced stages, her options are severely limited and her chances of stopping him could be all but gone.

I urge you to look at alcohol differently. This is not just a harmless recreational beverage, but a potent drug that can become a tool for rapists.

Reality Check: You don't have to drink, take drugs, or be sexually active to have friends and a happy social life.

If your personal morals or code of behavior would keep you celibate and sober, don't let anyone pressure you to betray your own principles. Women who don't drink and don't sleep around obviously are less likely to be caught in a potential rape situation, but never believe that it can't happen to you.

Dulled Senses

When you go out with a guy, you will have to depend on your feelings. Pay attention to the inexplicable instincts that tell you at times:

"Watch out!"

"There's something wrong with him!"

"He's not treating me with respect!"

"I don't feel comfortable with him anymore!"

"I'm starting to feel afraid. I want to go home!"

"I think I've made a terrible mistake!"

In many cases of sexual assault, the victim had a feeling something was going to happen or that the perpetrator was going to hurt her. There may be times when his behavior is not obvious enough for her to put her finger on why he makes her uncomfortable—she may have a "nagging feeling" that something is wrong with him. She may have thought she was being silly and brushed off her feelings with: *Oh, this is nonsense. He comes from a good family. He's an upper-classman. He's an honor student. He's so good looking. He's so popular. I should feel honored to be out with him.* Alcohol consumption may confuse the validity of the inner voice, while making it difficult to take appropriate defensive maneuvers. She may have ignored her instincts and gone ahead with his plans for the evening. This decision can be a dangerous mistake.

Garbled Communication

All successful relationships are based on communication. In a dating situation, the woman may not have had much time to get to know the man yet. It can be dangerous to be coy, vague, or subtle. A woman must be absolutely clear and precise in what she wants from the date and what she expects from the relationship. This may seem like cold and manipulative behavior, but the consequences of poor understanding and bad communication can be devastating.

The woman's words, body language, and gestures are all that she has to get the point across to the man. Alcohol tends to garble people's words and heavy drinking also affects the hearing. You may have noticed that when people get drunk, they tend to raise their voices. This is not only because some of their inhibitions are gone, but because the alcohol causes their hearing to become less acute.

Confusion and Disorientation

Alcohol affects the brain. It alters reality and changes the way you perceive what's going on around you. It makes reality less uncomfortable, but also can produce confusion and disorientation.

Confusion can become a major barrier to getting out of a dangerous acquaintance rape situation. You already are confused because you thought you knew this guy. You do not understand why he is doing this to you. You may not believe or refuse to believe what is happening to you because it is so unexpected. This sense of denial that you feel can seriously delay your defensive actions—if you can't accept what is happening to you, then you won't do anything to stop it or try to escape.

Rape can happen to anyone, and yes it can happen to you!

You may be saying to yourself, "Rape only happens in cities, to other people, with strangers who jump out of bushes. Rape doesn't happen to college students who come from good families; who are respectable and don't sleep around. Rapists are not good looking guys with 4.0 grade point averages. Rapists are not upperclassmen. Rapists are not fraternity brothers who are supposed to take care of you. Rape can't happen to me, can it?" Yes! Yes! Yes!

You may be saying rape only happens to young girls, to young women who are attractive and desirable. Rapists are not middle aged men, successful businessmen, lawyers, doctors, ministers. Rape can't happen to me, I'm middle aged. I'm divorced. I'm widowed. I'm not beautiful. It can't happen, can it? Yes! Yes! Yes!

All of these preconceived notions are major causes of confusion during an acquaintance rape situation. Adding alcohol raises the victim's confusion even more. Alcohol also may add to feelings of disorientation that she already may be experiencing as a new college student getting used to a new environment, new roommate/s, and new rules and restrictions.

Often when an acquaintance rape occurs, the victim is brought to a strange place. She may feel trapped and lost, not knowing how to get home or even get out of there. She may feel dependent for guidance and/or transportation on the man or men accompanying her, even if they are actually going to rape her. This feeling of being trapped is difficult enough to deal with without adding alcohol.

Impeded Self-Defense

Alcohol saps your strength, making you weaker than you normally are. To fend off a physical or sexual attack by a man or men takes a tremendous amount of strength. He is probably bigger, taller, and stronger than you, and although most date rape situations do not involve the use of a lethal weapon by the rapist, the size, weight, and strength of his body is weapon enough. You may have to kick him, slap him, run from him, or do any combination of things that could possibly deter him. You will need all your strength.

He will probably not be drinking as much as you because he knows he will need his strength to take advantage of you later. During a date rape, you have two enemies—the rapist, and the alcohol or drugs you have consumed.

Complicated Prosecution

There are many people, some of them unfortunately in the law enforcement and legal profession, who still believe that if you drink alcohol with someone and he ends up raping you, you asked for it. This is not true of course, but it has been a prevalent attitude. However, many people in law enforcement and the legal profession are starting to come around, finally changing their attitudes about blaming the victim for the rape.

Even if you drank to excess, you must remember that no one, no sane person, ever asks to be raped. There is only one person who is responsible for the crime of rape, and that is the rapist.

Reality Check: Blaming the rape victim only serves to sanction rape as a justifiable form of male behavior.

Rape is the only crime in which society tends to blame the victim and this is especially true when it comes to date rape. It is impossible to overstate the lack of sensitivity you may get from some men and women in law enforcement and in the courts if you have been drinking or taking drugs prior to the rape. They simply may not believe you or be willing to prosecute.

In one small town in Michigan, a college girl was raped by her date. The college believed her, but a local district attorney refused to prosecute because she had consumed one drink with the man three hours earlier.

Unfortunately, the only way to avoid this problem is to abstain from drinking completely. If you are having any sense that you may be in danger, consider refusing alcohol.

Even if you are dealing with sympathetic law enforcement officers, alcohol consumption may make it more difficult for you to remember what happened. You even may have become unconscious or blacked out. It is not uncommon for a woman to wake up after an assault with a sensation or feeling that something has happened to her, even though she does not remember the details. If you should ever awaken with a sense that you've been physically violated—but you cannot remember the incident—go to a rape crisis center or medical facility immediately for a medical exam.

The Rape Myth

Alcohol gives some men the idea that you can be manipulated and controlled if only they can get you drunk enough. Remember one of the most romantic scenes in the movie *Gone With the Wind* where Rhett Butler has been drinking, supposedly because his wife Scarlet is in love with another man. When he sees her, he threatens to tear her head off. She rebukes him and starts for the stairs. He runs over to her, grabs her against her will, and carries her up the long sweeping staircase, saying that this is one night she won't lock him out of her room. The next morning, Scarlet wakes up with a glowing smile on her face. Rhett, however, shows no caring or concern for her and announces that he intends to leave for London. This scene also illustrates the fact that alcohol is often used by men to give them the courage to do what their consciences would normally prohibit.

Rape? I know it sounds as though I just destroyed a great American classic. But we are led to believe in this scenario that the man raped a woman and she enjoyed it. Notice how it was alcohol that allowed Rhett Butler to overcome his inhibitions and get what he wanted. Perhaps you are saying that they were married—doesn't that make it acceptable? Absolutely not. This kind of scenario is all too common in many films and stories.

The myth is that it is acceptable for a man to use force to get a women into bed. She will resist a little and then she will just relax and enjoy it. There is a rampant idea on the part of some men that all women want to be taken. If a young man was raped against his will by another man, it would increase his awareness of the agony and horror of rape.

Some men still believe that women "want" to be raped, perhaps not consciously, but in their subconscious. They think that a woman wants to be overpowered and subdued. It is true that some people do have fantasies about being overpowered by someone who is strong, confident, and self-assured, but this is nothing more than a very human desire at times to have someone else take control. It is only a fantasy, and it has nothing to do with the reality of rape. No one in her right mind ever wants or asks to be raped.

Reality Check: Even within a marriage, if the woman does not want sex, and the man forces it on her, that is rape.

Once when discussing the writing of this book in a social setting, one man's immediate concern (and this is more common than you think), was, "What about the girl who teases a guy and gets him all turned on and then changes her mind? What about the girl who has sex with him and then the next morning decides to get even with the guy by claiming she was raped?" This statement that some men and women invariably bring up is, in my opinion, a learned defense mechanism against giving women power. It is apparent that many men do not want to take real responsibility for their own sexual behavior. For a man or anyone else to say that women invent being raped to get even with someone shows how little they know of the trauma, humiliation, and horror for the victim. Unsubstantiated charges of rape would appear to be a minuscule number in comparison with the actual rapes that are reported, especially considering most rapes are never reported. According to the FBI, only 8 percent of violent crimes reported (including rapes) have been found to be unsubstantiated reports.[9]

Date Rape Drugs

Ten years ago, alcohol was the most dangerous enabler in the date/acquaintance rape crime. Drugs, although dangerous and deadly, were not as easily obtainable, whereas alcohol was cheap and in plentiful supply. Today, alcohol is still the largest contributor to an acquaintance rape situation, but drugs are becoming more common and more problematic. Drugs like marijuana, cocaine, and other chemicals have some of the same abilities as alcohol to increase confusion and reduce a woman's ability to resist her attacker. In October 1996, the U.S. Congress passed a federal law increasing the penalties up to twenty years in prison for possession of a controlled substance with intent to commit a violent crime. What this amounts to is that a man using a drug to facilitate a date rape may face federal penalties as well as state sanctions.

There are three new narcotics on the scene, all of which cause a loss of muscle control and consciousness that are a danger to women, especially if they are administered to her without the woman's knowledge (i.e., in a spiked drink). These drugs are Rohypnol, GHB, and Ketamine.

Rohypnol (Flunitrazepam)

Rophies, Ruffies, Roofies, La Rocha, Roofenal, Roche, R2, Mexican Valium, Rib, Rope

Rohypnol is a powerful sedative commonly prescribed as a sleeping pill in Europe and Latin America since 1975. It is illegal in the United States. The tablets manufactured in Mexico (the source for most of the U.S. supply) are round, white, and slightly smaller than an aspirin. The manufacturer's markings are similar to those found on other pills, including Rivotril and Valium.

The drug causes drowsiness, loss of inhibition and judgment, dizziness, confusion, and in cases of high dosage, amnesia. "The drug's effects can begin within minutes," said Ann Marie Anglin, a spokesperson for Hoffmann-La Roche, the manufacturer of Rohypnol. Also, the drug's effects are intensified when used in conjunction with alcohol. Rohypnol is smuggled into the U.S. primarily from Colombia and Mexico in tablet form, according to U.S. Drug Enforcement Agency documents.[10] The tablets dissolve easily in beverages such as soft drinks, beer, and liquor, leaving no taste, color, or odor. "Rohypnol is becoming the drug of choice for would-be rapists whose identity is often masked by the amnesia-like effects of the drug," said Pamela Smith, a registered nurse at Boynton Health Service's Women's Clinic in Minneapolis. "There are women found in cars without clothes on who couldn't remember anything except that they feel violated," she said. Anecdotal reports indicate Rohypnol use is growing among high school students in the South, where it is seen as a cheap high at $.50 to $3 per pill. Because it is sold in a bubble pack, it can be mistaken for a legal substance. Continued use can result in addiction.

Until the summer of 1998, there was no testing available to determine the presence of Rohypnol in a person's bloodstream, however, anecdotes began multiplying in law enforcement agencies of young women reporting incidents in which they seemed to have lost consciousness and were then sexually assaulted. On reviving, they seemed to have no recollection of the incidents leading up to the assault, and in some cases, no knowledge of whom their assailants might be.

To help identify victims of Rohypnol-related sexual assaults and to combat negative press reports, Hoffmann-La Roche began offering free drug testing for suspected rape victims. Possible victims can have their urine tested for free within seventy-two hours of exposure at a public health care facility.

The use of Rohypnol in sexual assaults began in Florida and Texas, but quickly spread north. Health authorities at Penn State University in the town of State College, Pennsylvania, reported as many as ten suspected Rohypnol-related rapes in one semester since the drug test became available. Hoffmann-La Roche is cooperating with the Drug Enforcement Administration and other law enforcement agencies to stop illegal diversions of the drug into the United States. In late 1998, the company discontinued production of the potent two-milligram tablets, which appeared to be the dosage of choice among rapists.

GHB (Gamma hydroxybutyrate)
Liquid Extasy, Grievous Bodily Harm

GHB appears to be the latest in the constantly changing and trendy club and party drug scene. GHB, like many other drugs du jour, has been around for a long time—it was developed in the 1980s as a surgical anesthetic, but then it became popular as a muscle-building and weight-loss potion.

When combined with alcohol, GHB acts like a sedative and has had the effect on potential rape victims of causing unconsciousness, memory loss, and persistent tiredness. The sometimes unpredictable effects of GHB, along with its potential to cause vertigo, reduced heart rate, seizures, respiratory failure, and even coma, prompted the government to ban its use and sale, except for licensed research. GHB is commonly used with other drugs, including X (Extasy). Such use clouds both certainty about GHB's effects, and whether serious incidents associated with GHB were caused by that drug, or its combination with other substances. GHB seems to be particularly dangerous when mixed with alcohol.

GHB is often called "Liquid Extasy" because it comes in small bottles, with a capful of GHB providing users with X-like desires to be "touchy-feely," however, its overall impact is likened more to that of LSD than Extasy. This makes sense because GHB is a psychedelic sleep-inducer, whereas X is an amphetamine. GHB is a powerful sedative that can leave the body limp and tired. X is frequently taken along with GHB to counteract this sedation.

Ketamine
Special K, Ketalar, Ketaject, Super-K

Ketamine also has been used in date rape situations, causing the victim to become detached, confused, and uncoordinated. Clear thinking and communication are both impaired under the influence of this drug. Ketamine is closely related to PCP, and it produces very similar effects. Like PCP, Ketamine use produces a reaction called a dissociative state, and also like PCP, Ketamine is known to cause bad reactions in some of its users. However, unlike PCP, Special K is a legal prescription drug intended for use as an anesthetic for people and large animals. In recent years, Ketamine has begun to be used recreationally. Mixing this drug with alcohol is very dangerous.

Prevention Tips for Alcohol and Date Rape Drugs

• Do not drink to excess, or don't drink at all.

• Do not take "recreational" drugs, i.e., any drugs that are not pre-scribed to you by a physician, and don't mix any drugs with alcohol.

• In a restaurant or bar, turn your drink glass over to send the message to the waiter that you are not drinking.

• Do not drink if you are underage.

• If you do drink or take drugs, know your limit and avoid mixed drinks and/or mixing alcohol and drugs. Even prescription and over-the-counter drugs can be dangerous when mixed with alcohol.

• Avoid parties where excessive drinking and/or drug-taking is likely to occur.

• Never leave your drink unattended.

• Don't give your drink to someone else to watch.

• If you suspect that someone has put something in your drink, do not drink it. Get out of there at once.

• Alcohol and drugs are the single worst substances that can be added to a potential rape situation. If you drink, drink responsibly and don't let anyone pour your drink or allow anyone else to hold it.

chapter seven

the four personalities of the rapist

Before you accept any generic crime prevention or self-defense advice, you should remember that there are three factors that will determine your ability to escape an attacker.

First, your response to the assault depends on your personality. You only can be successful if your response is practical. By that I mean that if you are told to scream, kick, fight, and act very aggressively, it will only work if your personality is not passive and shy. Conversely, if you are assertive and bold by nature, acting passive may not be possible for you. Your response will be more effective if it matches your personality.

Second, your response needs to be practical in terms of location. For example, screaming will be a waste of time in an isolated spot, where no one can hear you, while you can take advantage of some locations, like a parking lot where you can crawl under a parked car.

The third and probably most important is this: Your response needs to take into consideration the personality type of the perpetrator. We, as a society, have a hard time thinking of attractive people as being danger-ous. We have been conditioned by the media to think of rapists and other violent criminals as twisted, evil degenerates who are always repulsive and obnoxious. They are never like us or like the guy next door.

Reality Check: Rapists and other criminals come in all sizes and shapes, and rarely conform to the media's stereotypes.

We know that not all rapists are alike. They operate differently and are motivated by different factors. The goal for the rapist is not sex, but power. Rapists seem to lack a sense of inner power. They may have a great deal of rage at all women, and that may be triggered by an incident with a specific woman from the past.

Reality Check: Most rapists are white and choose victims within their own race who live and work near their own home. Most rapists are not lower class working people but middle-class, educated men.[11]

According to the FBI Behavioral Sciences Unit and many experts in criminal psychology, there are four different types of personalities in men who commit rape. It is important that women understand that these are general patterns which may not apply to any one particular individual. The following illustration will indicate who the most common rapists are and who is getting all of the media attention.

Diagram 2: Four personality types of rapists

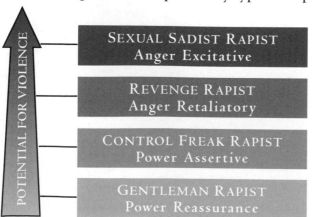

SEXUAL SADIST RAPIST
Anger Excitative

REVENGE RAPIST
Anger Retaliatory

CONTROL FREAK RAPIST
Power Assertive

GENTLEMAN RAPIST
Power Reassurance

POTENTIAL FOR VIOLENCE

Gentleman Rapist (Power Reassurance)

The vast majority, 70 percent, of reported rapes are committed by men with Power Reassurance personalities. This kind of person is the most common type of date/acquaintance rapist and is often called the "Gentleman Rapist" because of his "gentlemanly" behavior after the rape. As the name indicates, the Power Reassurance rapist is less violent and less sure of himself. He seeks power and gets it through sex, or rape. He rarely carries a weapon, and will often use coercion or the threat of violence to get control of his intended sexual partner. He doesn't consider his own behavior to be rape, and will be shocked when he learns that he has been accused of rape. He believes in a fantasy of the encounter, actually thinking that he and the victim have just had a good time together. He will offer to drive or walk his victim home after the crime, and express concern for her safety. He most often will expect his victim to continue the "relationship" that he has started, and may ask her out again the following night.

Robin Warshaw writes in *I Never Called it Rape*,

> *Some acquaintance rapists become oddly tender immediately afterward and try to dress the woman or cover them [sic]. Some gallantly insist on walking or driving their victims home, telling the woman that it's dangerous for them to be out alone. Others profess love and talk about having an ongoing relationship. Another type kisses their victims good-bye and says they will call them again soon. (And some do call, apparently raring to go on another "date.") In short, many men fail to perceive what has just happened as rape.*

The Power Reassurance rapist may fantasize about having a relationship with his victim long before he ever gets her alone and will be planning to have sex with her very early in the relationship. *He is the classic date rapist.* Because he rarely uses a weapon, and doesn't generally inflict additional physical injury on his victim, he often will get the sympathy of those who know him. His mild manner on the surface, however, hides rage and a determination to get what he wants. He can cross-over to become a

Revenge Rapist or a Sexual Sadist and is just as dangerous, perhaps even more so, because he will most likely get away with his crime and do it again.

The man who commits date/acquaintance rape tends to be more selective in his victims and is more influenced by social standards of beauty—his victim is usually someone whom he would normally wish to date. He often will believe that he is being a man and that taking a woman by force is his right, an attitude that society seems to reinforce. The history of the media in this country is filled with movies, books, magazines, stories, television, and music videos that either condone or promote violence and rape. As mentioned earlier, even a classic such as *Gone With the Wind* may promote the traditional idea that men have the right of conquest over women and that after the assault a woman will thank the man and then reward him with her love. Although the motion picture and television industries have come a long way in terms of rape/violence messages, today's music and music videos are among the most violent and contain the most virulent anti-female messages that have ever been seen or heard. These media messages reinforce the attitudes towards women that may cause some men to commit rape.

Prevention: As the most common of all rapists, and often the most respectable in society's eyes, this personality type is seldom seen as a criminal. The best way to break through to escape is to be assertive with him. You must make him understand that what he's about to do is not love, not sex, not fun, it's rape! Attempt to break through his fantasy by screaming, fighting, or otherwise actively resisting him. Try to make him understand that what he is doing is a crime.

Control Freak (Power Assertive)

In 25 percent of all rape reports, the control freak personality surfaces. This personality tends to be found in a white male in his mid-twenties with a blue collar job, who has the freedom to travel. This kind of rapist is more violent than the Gentleman Rapist and he may initiate a sudden attack. He may carry a weapon, and he doesn't care about his victim. He will tend to be cruel to others and domineering in his attitude, often insisting that others do things his way. He may insist on ordering for a woman in a reataurant and will discourage her from having ideas and opinions of her own. He has often been called the Dr. Jeckyl and Mr. Hyde rapist, because he may suddenly change in personality and appearance if he becomes threatened. His level of violence can escalate and his personality become that of the Revenge Rapist or Sexual Sadist at any time. This personality is generally the easiest to identify prior to the attack. He will often reveal his true personality early on in the relationship. His tendency is not to see a woman as a real person, and he will talk about women derisively and in a way that objectifies them.

Prevention: Talk to him, getting eye contact and making yourself real to him. There have been more than a few cases of rapists changing their minds when their victims were able to make a connection with someone the rapist really cared about, such as a sister or mother. Talk about yourself and try to make him see you as a unique and real person.

Revenge Rapist (Anger Retaliatory)

Although only 4 percent of reported rapes can be traced to this personality type, it gets a lot of media attention. As the label indicates, there is anger here and this man is retaliating against women. Usually a white male, in his early thirties, he tends to be educated and somewhat successful, which enables him to travel extensively, making capture more difficult. This personality type may strike quickly with a high level of violence. Generally, there is a precipitating event that triggers rage, such as in the David Berkowitz case (the "Son of Sam"), who was triggered by family quarrels. This type of rapist's victims tend to be similar. He often takes a possession, or "trophy," from his victims. Although he may not originally intend to kill, he often does.

Prevention: If confronted by this type of rapist, you are in great danger. This man harbors a great deal of hatred and rage. Your best bet is to attempt to escape, fighting with all your might and trying not to let him get you to an isolated spot.

Sexual Sadist (Anger Excitative)

Only 1 percent of all reported rapists fall into this category, and these tend to be stranger-to-stranger rapes, or an acquaintance rape in which the victim and perpetrator had only just met. The very term indicates that this individual is angry and gets excited by the thrill of the crime. He intends to kill his victim. He will plan extensively, and counts on the intended victim to provide him with an opportunity. He tends to be a white male in his thirties or forties, and is generally well educated.

Ted Bundy falls into the category of a sexual sadist. His Volkswagen Beetle was always prepared for a kidnapping, with the right side passenger seat removed and a tire iron stored in the back. He also carried around duct tape and handcuffs. Bundy's modus operandus was to lure victims to him by pretending he was helpless. He often wore a cast on his leg or arm. He was so good looking that when he asked a young female to help him with a box that he was struggling with, he would invariably get her to drop her guard and get close. Ted Bundy counted on his intended victims to be vulnerable and trust him. It is believed he was responsible for killing over thirty young girls and women.

Denial is so rampant that even when the facts are presented, many can't bring themselves to believe an attractive man can rape. During Bundy's trial, several women attended the proceedings wanting to have a relationship with him. As sick as it sounds, even up to his death some of these women wanted him to be their friend, lover, or mate.

Prevention: If you are attacked by this kind of person, you can bet that you will have to fight like hell to get away. Since this type of individual is very clever, your best bet is to be aware and trust that inner guidance that tells you not to get too close or be alone with him. If you carry some kind of weapon, you must be prepared to use it at a moment's notice.

**Reality Check: Remember that all rapists are serial rapists.
That is, they rape repeatedly until stopped.**

Rapists rarely stop themselves. The vast majority of rapists have access to sex and what they're really after is not sex, but power. They tend to have a low sense of self-esteem and this is their way of being powerful. They may have an addiction to the feelings of power and excitement that they experience from committing their crimes.

The real issue in rape prevention education is the increasing prevalence of rage. Some men perceive their power base is being eroded by women, and some men may strike back at women in general by attacking particular women.

It is important to understand that rapists seldom fit neatly into one category or another. Often, there are traits from more than one personality type present. A rapist also can progress by degrees from one category to another. It some cases, the rapist will get increasingly violent as his crimes continue because the excitement of the rape dissipates and he increases the violence to add to the excitement.

Although a rapist may progress to greater violence as time goes on, at this time, there is insufficient evidence to indicate that any particular acquaintance rapist will escalate to more violent or homicidal behavior.

What Turns an Ordinary Man into a Rapist?

What turns an ordinary man into a date/acquaintance rapist? In many cases, it's a simple case of opportunity. If the opportunity exists, and the man thinks he won't get caught, he'll take it. In fact, a recent study by a major university indicated that a very alarming percentage of college and high school males would rape if they thought no one would ever find out.[12] Although this book is an attempt to get women to be alert to the potential dangers in dating as well as all social situations, it is also a "cry in the wilderness" for men to stop their rage against women. For some people, the assumption is that if women would change their behavior, men might stop raping. That is not the case. *If a woman changes her behavior and becomes more alert to the dangers around her, the best she can hope for is that the attacker will choose another victim.* No matter what women do, some men will continue to rape.

The fact is that whether a woman is raped by a stranger or by someone she knows, she still has been violated. The pain is the same, the hurt is the same, the feeling of having her innocence stripped away is the same. The trauma can be more intense when a woman is raped by her date/acquaintance or "friend," because she had an unspoken bond of trust with him. She knows strangers are dangerous, but when friends, dates, lovers, or husbands become rapists, who can she trust? Who is her enemy?

Until men are re-educated about a women's right to her own body and sexual activities, this problem will continue. Education, unfortunately, takes time. For now, teens and women have to be alert, aware, and conscious that they can become a target for a man's violence.

It's All About Power

Why do men rape? And why do they rape women they know? Society has misunderstood the method and modality of the rapist. We think we can understand a young attractive woman being raped, but not a child, and not an older woman. Not until we understand that rape is about power, will we understand the rape or the rapist. Date rape or acquaintance rape is a violent act of control perpetrated, not by a sick inhuman animal, but by an average guy who, *given the right circumstances and the right frame of mind*, may commit rape. It even may be that he would never consider himself a rapist.

In general, if you ask a man if he has ever raped a woman, he will of course say he has not. But ask him again if he has ever had sex with someone against her will, when she apparently did not want to participate. You will be amazed at the number of men who will say that indeed they have had sex under these circumstances. In addition, a man's behavior may change with the situation. Although it may appear as a spontaneous act, many times, date rapes are not. In some cases, plans are made and people or potential witnesses are gotten rid of to make the situation safe for the rapist and unsafe for the intended victim.

Reality Check: When you are confronted with a man who intends to rape you, you must assume the very worst in order for you to respond effectively.

However well you may have thought you knew this man, he is now your enemy and your life is in danger. Quickly act to protect yourself, following your instincts. Remember, if you escape or even if you just survive, then you did the right thing.

Stranger Rape

Stranger rape is primarily an act of violence to control, in which the attacker attempts to humiliate and degrade the victim. The purpose of this kind of rape is to gain power through intimidation. In *The Gift of Fear*, Gavin de Becker outlines the conclusions of his research on the techniques that criminals often use to prey upon women. These techniques are similar to, but are different in degree from, the warning signs that a date rapist might exhibit. If you observe a man using one or more of these techniques, you should be on your guard and get away from him quickly. Do not allow yourself to be alone with him, and do not hesitate or analyze. Act quickly to protect yourself.

Criminal Techniques

Forced Teaming: This is a tactic of manipulation in which the man attempts to create a "shared purpose or experience" where none exists. The man refers to the woman and himself as "we," even if they have just met, and even when it is highly inappropriate, attempting to make the woman feel that he and she are sharing a common pursuit or purpose.

Prevention: When you notice this kind of behavior, ask yourself, "Why is he trying to create a team of the two of us?" Remind yourself that you and he are not sharing an experience, and remain on your guard.

Charm and Niceness: "To charm is to compel or control by allure or attraction," says de Becker. Rather than thinking that a man is charming, a woman should say to herself, "This man is trying to charm me." Many women who have been assaulted report that the man was extremely "nice" at the beginning. Beware of behavior that is excessive, inappropriate, or seems dazzling.

Prevention: If you have a sense that a man is exhibiting behavior that is unusual for the situation, ask yourself, "Why might he be acting so nicely?" or, "Why would he be trying to charm me?"

Too Many Details: It is common for a person who is lying to offer too many details in an effort to bolster his credibility. A person who is telling the truth is not preoccupied with whether or not he is being believed, while a person who is lying will work hard to be convincing.

Prevention: If you are hearing a mass of details or background information that you did not solicit, you should ask yourself, "Why is he trying to convince me?" Try not to get too distracted by the story so that you can remain alert and clear about what is really going on.

Typecasting: A common maneuver is to make a slightly critical statement that then challenges the listener to prove the opposite. The man does not necessarily believe what he is saying, he only believes that his statement will affect the woman's behavior. For example, he might say, "You're so well dressed that you're probably really uptight and wouldn't know how to have a good time." The woman may find herself trying to prove to him that she does know how to have a good time, and may go along with things she otherwise wouldn't in order not to be perceived as "uptight."

Prevention: The best way to counteract this tactic is to say nothing, and not to take the bait. If you find yourself thinking, "I'll show him I'm not uptight," you are falling into his trap.

Any one of the above maneuvers may be used to attempt to control or manipulate a woman into a situation in which the assailant has power over her. Power is so much the focus of the exercise, that in a stranger rape situation, copulation often is not completed. The turn-on for the rapist is the conquest of power, not sex. This sometimes escalates into further and further acts of violence against the victim. Stranger rape can be compared to an addict's drug habit. As his addiction increases, his need also increases for more drugs (or in this case, violence) to achieve the same high. Some rapists need to hurt their victim a little more with each assault until the only thing that gives them their "high" is to kill.

This kind of criminal eventually may become obsessed with the thrill of killing his victim and will increase the frequency of his crime until he is caught or stopped. He does not, in many cases, wait for the right circumstances to commit his crime, and will often go to great lengths to create the ideal situation. To this kind of criminal, age, race, sex, or physical characteristics mean nothing.

Gang Rape

According to the U.S. Department of Justice, gang rape accounts for about 9 percent of all reported rapes.[13] However, the physical and emotional damage that is inflicted upon the victim of a gang rape is enormous. In *Against Our Will,* Susan Brownmiller writes: "When men rape in pairs or gangs, the sheer physical advantage of their position is clear-cut and unquestionable. No simple conquest of man over woman, group rape is the conquest of men over Woman."

Often, men who commit gang rape normally would be too timid to perpetrate a rape by themselves. When they become part of a group of men, this changes, particularly if there has been a great deal of alcohol consumed. Men who commit gang rape experience a special bonding and there seems to be a sense of pride in humiliating their victim. They prove their manhood and standing in the group. Generally, the group leader is the first to commit rape and the others will then follow. It is also true that part of the motivation for the members of the gang is to not lose status or look bad in front of the others.

Gang rape is generally much more violent and abusive than normal date and acquaintance rape. The perpetrators of gang rape appear to have a lot of hostility and rage against women and, if prosecuted, will go to great lengths to deny the incident and accuse the victim. Gang rapes are more common at events where alcohol and drugs are consumed. Fraternity parties and athletic parties can be a breeding ground for this kind of assault.

Prevention: If all else fails, and you find yourself being assaulted by a group of men, try to make eye contact with one person. Tell him to go get help. You may be able to break the male-bonding with him long enough for him to feel compassion for you. Depending on his personality and the group's control over him, it may or may not work. Above all, remember that, regardless of the circumstances, the attack is not your fault.

chapter eight

the ABCs of date rape

There are three factors that make up the ABCs of date rape. They are *Agenda*, *Belief*, and *Communication*. Not all date and acquaintance rapes are pre-planned acts of violence. They may end up there, but many start as miscommunication and faulty belief systems that add to the problem of understanding the opposite sex.

In chapter four, I discussed the Date Rape Triangle, the three factors that exist at the time of almost all sexual assaults taking place in a dating situation. In this chapter, I want to discuss the broader social context as it applies to date rape, and as I have interpreted it from hundreds of conversations with attendees at my Date Rape Prevention seminars. The topics in this chapter are broad in scope and are the realm of sociologists, who have many different views on societal shifts. It is important for women, however, to take into consideration the context in which their dating experiences are occurring. Such awareness decreases a woman's vulnerability. It also may allow for an individual woman to see more clearly how an individual man might pose a potential danger to her, and to take the necessary steps to protect herself.

First of all, it must be seen that, in spite of many advances for women over the past few decades, women are still pervasively discriminated against and experience inequity in many areas of life. There is a great deal of ambivalence throughout our society about gender roles and differences. Many women who view themselves as equals to men run into men who resist this view. Boys and girls still are raised with markedly different attitudes, resulting in apparent "innate" differences in adult men and women. The popularity of such books as *Men are from Mars, Women are from Venus* by John Gray and *You Just Don't Understand* by Deborah Tannen attest to the widely held notion that there may be fundamental differences in men and women. Many women's advocates object to the notion that there are inherent gender differences because, for so many years, these differences have been cited as a way to justify gender discrimination. Yet, many mothers will tell you that their sons and daughters appear to come into the world with different predilections and inborn interests.

At the very least, it is fair to say that certain aspects that may be present in all people are emphasized in people's upbringing depending on their gender. For example, while all people may be inclined toward independence and competitiveness to some degree, these qualities are encouraged in boys, and while all people need cooperation and relatedness, these are emphasized in girls. When these boys and girls grow up to be adults and begin to seek each other out both romantically and sexually, there may be marked differences in their agendas, belief systems, and communication modes. The clash of these elements may result in date rape.

Again, while it is ultimately up to men to stop all rape—and I encourage men to grapple with the ABCs of date rape—I believe it is imperative for a woman to ascertain the agenda of her date, to explore his belief system, to look for the qualities that many rapists share, and to use the most effective communication she can to remain safe from sexual assault.

A = Agenda

Men's Agenda

Many men have a different agenda from women in relationships. If men and women both wanted the same things in a relationship, there would be far less miscommunication. However, this is not usually the case. When a man is in his early years, from age seventeen to twenty-five, he may be preoccupied with sex—it may be on his mind constantly.

A man may think that women exist for only one reason—to have sex with him. This time in his life may be filled with doubts about his own masculinity, frustration, fear, and a strong need to be accepted by his peers. He may feel that the only way to prove his manhood to himself and his peers is by having sex. Locker-room talk reflects this need on the part of young men to prove their importance through sexual conquest.

Reality Check: Sex, or the ability to have sex with a woman, should have nothing to do with a secure, healthy man's sense of self-worth.

Erik Johnke, a male student at Haverford College, described the gender role-playing that goes on between a man and a woman on a date. The following is taken from his senior thesis as quoted in *I Never Called it Rape* by Robin Warshaw.

The man is taught to look upon his actions on a date as a carefully constructed strategy for gaining the most territory. Every action is evaluated in terms of the final goal—intercourse. He continually pushes to see "how far he can get."

Every time she (his date) submits to his will, he has "advanced" and every time she does not, he has suffered a "retreat." Since he already sees her as the opponent, and the date as a game or a battle, he anticipates resistance.

He knows that "good girls don't," and so she will probably say "no." But he has learned to separate himself from her and her interests. He is more concerned with winning the game. Instead of trying to communicate with her, he attempts to pressure her into saying "yes."

Every time she submits to his will, he sees it as a small victory (getting the date, buying her a drink, getting a kiss, or fondling her breasts). He plays upon her indecisiveness, using it as an opportunity to tell her "what she really wants," which is, in fact, what he wants. If her behavior is inconsistent, he tells her that she is "fickle" or "a tease." If he is disinterested in her desires and believes that she is inconsistent, he is likely to ignore her even when she does express her desires directly. When she finally says, "No," he simply may not listen, or he may convince himself that she is just "playing hard to get" and that she really means "yes." With such a miserable failure of communication, a man can rape a woman even when she is resisting vocally and physically, and still believe that it was not rape.

Reality Check: A date or a relationship should not be a contest, game, or battlefield. It is a chance for two people to get to know each other.

Women's Agenda

Women may want different things from relationships than men do—this is especially true in the early years. As men and women get older, they tend to become more alike and share the same wants, needs, and goals in their relationships and lives. But in the teenage and early adult years (ages sixteen to thirty) they can be separated by vast differences. For women, relationships mean cooperation and support. They want companionship and friendship. They look for men who communicate and make them feel secure and safe. For them, communication is extremely important. They grow up sharing feelings, desires, dreams, and ambitions with their mothers and other females. When life is difficult, they get comfort and understanding through talking it out with a close friend. Men, when life gets difficult, may withdraw from communication.

Prevention: It is easy to see how this clash in agendas—men seeking sex, women seeking companionship—can lead to disastrous results. The safest thing for a woman in a younger age bracket is to assume that a man she's dating has sex on his agenda, and make her decisions accordingly. More mature women may be able to draw their conclusions after some communication has taken place. Although it may seem like an awkward thing to do, a woman would do well to discuss her own agenda for the date right at the outset of the evening.

B = Beliefs

Men's Beliefs

Many men have very distinct beliefs about men and women. They often believe that most women are manipulative, controlling, and generally don't know what they want. They are perplexed about women's emotional states most of the time, preferring logic to emotion, mainly because many men are trained from boyhood to express themselves through logic and to suppress their emotions. On the other hand, they want women's sexual favors. The old adage, *"Men give love to get sex,"* is still true for many men. Many men who commit rape perceive women as sexual teases who change their minds after getting the man excited. These men tend to believe that once they become sexually aroused, they have to copulate and cannot stop until it's over. These men may be capable of completely separating the act of sex from the emotion of love, and may see women as objects whose purpose is to serve men.

Some men with these kinds of beliefs believe that a husband cannot rape his wife and that she is the property of and belongs to her husband. They also may believe a man should be in strict control of finances and decisions in the home and that he is the head of the household. These beliefs are often reinforced by the world's major religions, which are based upon male dominance.

Fortunately, some men have been influenced by the women's movement and are beginning to view relationships as more equitable. This shift also may take place as a man reaches his thirties and forties and may begin to see the importance and appeal of a balanced relationship.

Women's Beliefs

Today, many women believe that all men want only one thing. This is especially true if they are young and dating younger men. They tend to think men are jerks, that they can't communicate, or won't share their feelings. They often don't feel men are very smart and are certainly not sensitive and caring.

Some women also feel men don't understand them and they are perplexed by men's unwillingness to talk and share. They see men often in roles of control and manipulation and resent their attitudes about women in general. Many women who have attended my seminars can't understand why any man would rape or assault someone, since they are not driven for power as men are. In spite of all this, they love men and look for a loving, caring, and supportive partner with whom to build a relationship. Most of these women see relationships as a "win/win" situation. They look for partners who will respect them and put time and work into the relationship. They are used to sharing their feelings and to experiencing enduring relationships with other females.

Many women need support and love and a feeling of safety before they give sexual favors. Emotional closeness is very important to them. The old adage, *"A woman gives sex to get love,"* remains true for many women.

For many women, having sexual intercourse is the most intimate and vulnerable situation they can be in, so a feeling of safety and emotional support is vital. Such a woman has a hard time separating sex from her feelings about the man with whom she is involved. In essence, she needs to be loved and cherished and made to feel special before she feels comfortable having sexual contact.

Prevention: A woman must ascertain early on the extent to which the man she is dating believes that women are inferior to men. She must both listen closely to his words and carefully observe his behavior. Remember that disparaging remarks about women along with inappropriately controlling behavior may be warning signals of a rapist.

C = Communication

Communication between men and women has become increasingly difficult as roles are in flux. Some men are confused today as to what women want and expect from them. Men and women may communicate differently, and for different reasons. It is beyond the scope of this book to argue whether this is learned or innate, it is just the reality with which we're dealing at this time. Date rape can start as a failure of communication.

Based on my experience with a wide range of people, for women, talk is the glue that holds relationships together, while for men, relationships are held together primarily by activities such as sports or politics. The situations in which men are most inclined to talk are those in which they feel the need to impress, in circumstances where their status is in question. Whereas women communicate to get cooperation and consensus, men tend to communicate to establish position and hierarchy. Men in general have difficulty talking unless there is some definite point to make or information to obtain. Women on the other hand communicate with greater ease and establish friendships and non-hierarchical groups.

Dr. David Viscott, in his book *I Love You, Let's Work it Out*, comments on the miscommunication about affection that often happens between men and women:

It is especially difficult for many men to understand that the warmth and friendship of just being together is as important as sex in the relationship. Without this closeness, most women feel cheated, unloved, and unwilling to be sexually involved although they may have sex in the hope that there will be a tender moment afterward. Unfortunately, if the tender moment is not there before, it is unlikely that it will be there later.

Affection is diminished when it is misread as an invitation for sex. Mostly it is men who misinterpret affectionate approaches. The woman, usually wanting closeness with sex far removed from her mind, reaches out to be affectionate to her mate and finds him suddenly aroused, thinking she wants to make love. This disappoints and hurts her and she pulls back. He accuses her of starting something she won't finish.

At this point, the man—if he's aggressive, determined, and if he feels that his manhood has been abused—may use force to finish what he thinks the woman started in the first place.

In a relationship, people need to communicate to establish closeness and a feeling of caring for each other. Women's great complaint is that men don't communicate. This is not true—they do communicate, but when they do, it is often non-verbally. Many men show their feelings not by words, but by deeds. If you want to effectively communicate with a man, do it in terms he's used to, not in words that he may not hear, but in actions.

Communication is much more than words. Only 7 percent of communication is verbal, while 38 percent is tone of voice, and 55 percent is body language. That means that in order to communicate effectively in a dating situation, a woman must use all three—words, tone of voice, and body language to get her point across. This is especially true if alcohol and drugs are being used.

Reality Check: You have to use all three means of communication— verbal, tone of voice, and body language—when you are communicating with a man on a date.

A major problem in date rape situations occurs if a woman is sending mixed messages, due either to ambivalence, a desire to be "nice," or some other reason. If she is saying, "No," but her tone of voice is not reinforcing that she means what she says, the man may not get the message. And if she is saying, "No," but her body language is not also saying, "No," he may instead believe what he wants to believe.

You may have spent the entire evening trying to tell your date that you were not interested in a sexual relationship, but he may not have heard you. He will however, understand your message if you do something physical. The simple act of removing your hand from his will get his attention much faster than gently dropping a verbal hint in an ongoing conversation.

Communication Through What You Wear

There is a lot of misinformation out there about the importance of what a woman wears in relation to her susceptibility to rape. In fact, statistics indicate that a victim's choice of apparel contributed to the rapist's decision to commit rape in only 3 percent of all rape cases. Yet, we are a visual society and people respond to what they see. Many men and women still believe that if a woman wears a provocative outfit, she's "asking for it." This is rarely the case! A woman may wear a provocative outfit to attract attention and be noticed, but attracting attention is not asking to be raped. If a man drives a flashy sports car, does that mean he's asking to be robbed? Of course not.

Reality Check: No matter what a woman wears, it does not give a man permission to molest, assault, or rape her. It is inappropriate to blame men's criminal behavior on the clothing worn by women.

What a woman wears does send messages, however, and if she is trying to be taken seriously and not as a sexual object, she needs to be conscious of the message she's sending. If you want to send a message to a man that says, "I am a woman who deserves to be treated with respect," then try sending the message visually through what you wear. Reinforce the visual message with words and actions. In this way, you are more likely to communicate what you want and he is more likely to get the message.

You also should understand that there are no guarantees, you may be dressed like a nun and still get raped.

So the key here is, wear what is comfortable and consistent with who you are and the message you are trying to send to the world. You have the right to walk around wearing as little or as much as you wish. However, everything we do has consequences. Wearing clothing that sends mixed signals to men might make it much harder for you to convince them that you're not easy prey. Someday, society will not blame women for what they wear, and men will not automatically assume that a provocative outfit

71

means you are looking for sex, but until that day comes, be alert to the kind of messages you're sending (whether or not they're intentional) and the kind of responses you're getting from others. If changing your wardrobe results in fewer problems with men, it might be worth the change.

The key in preventing date rape is to be consistent with all of the communication that you send. Your words, tone of voice, and body language should all be saying the same thing. That's effective communication. Great relationships are about effective and consistent communication. Start your relationship off to a good start by saying what you mean. Silence can lead to misinformation and assumptions. Speak up. Speak clearly. Say what's on your mind, and keep saying it until you know you have reached him. He can't read your mind, so don't expect him to.

One way to establish your independence right away is to approach each dating situation on equal ground. Insist on having your own transportation, and on paying your own expenses. Under these conditions, a woman is not as likely either to feel or be perceived to be obligated to a man. The man is also less likely to think that she owes him sexual favors since she spent her own money. This is especially a good idea when both parties do not know each other very well.

Seven Keys to Clear Communication

The clearer your communication is in a dating situation, the safer you are. Use the following seven techniques to protect yourself. (Understand that when you drink or take any kind of drugs, your ability to communicate clearly will be affected, both because your speech may become slurred and because you may not be focused enough to interpret signals that he is sending out as true warnings.)

1. Speak forcefully and clearly! This is no time for a weak squeaky voice. Try lowering your voice which sounds more authoritative.

2. Look him straight in the eye! We all have different ways of communicating and listening. Just saying the words without making eye con-

tact may not be enough. Establishing eye contact is one way to assure yourself that he has heard what you said.

3. Make sure he has heard you and understood you. Simple is better. Get some kind of acknowledgment from him. If he mumbles, ask him, *"Do you understand me?"*

4. Make sure he understands that he is—and you are not—responsible for his actions. You will know whether what you've said has made an impact by judging his actions. If he becomes immediately defensive by saying he can't stop if he gets turned on, then you must be more assertive about what you want out of the date.

5. Make sure he understands that you and you alone will decide if and when you participate in any sexual activity. You do have power. Many men believe that women are the "gate-keepers" of men's sexual pleasure. In reality, you hold the key only to your own sexual activity. He holds the key to his. You also can explain how much more fulfilling and wonderful the act of intercourse will be if both of you are ready and are in agreement about when to initiate sex into the relationship.

6. Let him know, in no uncertain terms, that failure to honor your wishes will result in severe consequences for him. Sometimes you have to go to extremes to communicate. Don't settle for something and someone you don't want. Do whatever it takes to get your point across. Don't get talked into going along to please him. He may say, "I love you. If you loved me you'd do it." You can always say, "If you really loved me, you wouldn't ask me to do something that I don't want to do."

7. Tell him, "After I say no, it's rape!" Non-consensual sex is rape, and sometimes you have to call it what it is. The vast majority of men to whom I've talked who have admitted to having sex with a woman when she didn't want to, would never identify their own actions as rape. They deny that they could ever do such a thing. If you are saying, "No," and not being heard, clearly state that you consider that he has no further right to touch or control you.

Specific Prevention Phrases

Following are some specific phrases or sentences you can use early in the evening, before any physical contact has taken place:

1. "I want you to know that I'm not interested in a physical relationship now, and I would appreciate it if you would honor my feelings and not pressure me at this point. OK?"

2. "I would feel more comfortable if we met each other at [a neutral location]. OK?"

3. "I want to drive my car because I feel safer that way. Please understand, this is no reflection on you. This is something I always do during the first few dates. OK?"

4. "I don't appreciate your statement about women. I am a woman too and when you talk about women, you are talking about me. If you want my respect, you must show me that you respect not only me, but all women as well. OK?"

5. "Is that a put down? If it is, I don't appreciate it. Please don't do that again. OK?"

Do not be afraid to pin him down for his comments. If you sit there and take it or say nothing, he may either assume that you agree with him or are too weak to confront him and that you will say nothing later if and when he begins to rape you.

You will notice that in statements 1 to 5, each statement is followed by you asking, "OK?" There is a good reason for this. You are asking for his acknowledgment and agreement with your desires and wishes. *You are not asking for his permission.* You also really want to know if he has heard you. Some men often turn women off in their heads and do not really listen to their words. This is not necessarily done with malice or even consciously, but often they are self-absorbed and not used to listening to women. You must be sure that your communication has been heard and understood. Later in the evening, if his behavior is in conflict with his earlier agreement with your wishes, he can be reminded of his agreement.

It is also the case that if he's drinking, he may not physically hear you, as people who drink can suffer some hearing loss.

6. "I'm feeling uncomfortable with your behavior. I want to go home. Please take me home right now."

7. "I'm going home. You don't have to drive me. I have my own car." [Or, "I am calling a friend to pick me up."]

8. "I don't feel like drinking. Please don't pressure me to drink when I don't want to."

You may indicate to him that you are not going to drink by turning your glass over or by telling the server that you will not be drinking tonight and asking that the wine glass be taken away. Involving the server is a good idea because you now have a witness that you did not drink or that you stopped drinking at some point in the evening.

I know that some of these techniques may sound extreme, especially in a dating situation, but it is better to sound strong and clear in your communication than to be silent or unclear and be perceived as weak and submissive.

chapter nine

what to do if you are confronted

Reality Check: There are no guarantees that rape will not happen to you no matter how careful you are and no matter how well-prepared you are.

Naturally, it is important to practice as much prevention as possible and that includes moderation of alcohol consumption and watching for any signs or danger signals that a man may be giving.

Rape is an act of violence and control, not an act of sex, love, or seduction. Even if you lose control in a dating situation, you may be able to regain what you've lost by re-establishing a strong line of direct communication. If communication does not work to avert the assault, you may need to resort to fighting back.

Verbal Self-Defense

First of all, try to talk to your assailant and be clear in your communication. The earlier in a dating situation your wishes are known to him, the more likely he will be to honor your desires or lack of desires for him.

As the situation escalates, he may either not believe you or think you are playing hard to get.

Your words are only 7 percent of your communication, 38 percent is the tone of your voice, and 55 percent of your communication is in your body language. Your tone of voice and your body language must match your words.

A man is more likely to believe your body language, or his perceptions of your body language than your words, especially if they are in conflict. Some men tend to believe that a woman doesn't know what she wants. If your communication is open to interpretation, the man may interpret it to his advantage and to your disadvantage.

If you are in a situation where you are alone with a man who is becoming sexually aggressive, you may succeed in averting the attack if you can:

• Try to stop the momentum long enough for him to look at you.

• Try to get him to think about what he is doing and the consequences of his actions.

• Try to get him to think about you as a person, not as an "object" that he must control or has the right to conquer.

Remember that he may not be listening to you so you need to communicate with strength and clarity. Make your statements strong. You may try to lower your voice since a high voice can sound weak and too feminine for him to take you seriously. He may tend to listen to you more if your voice is harder and stronger.

The following statements are suggestions that may work for you. There is no one statement or group of words that will work in all situations. Every situation is different. Use your instincts. Listen to that inner voice and let it guide you on how you can best reach this guy, and act quickly.

If you do not wish to accept his more physical advances, you may find some of these statements effective (these are only suggestions; put them into your own words if they don't sound right for you):

"Back off! I need my space!"

"Stop touching me. I don't want you to do that. Stop it now!"

"What you are doing is making me uncomfortable. Please stop it right now!"

"What do you think you're doing?"

"Are you trying to get me drunk so that you can take advantage of me?" (This is no joke, so do not let him humor or patronize you by not taking you seriously.)

"Why are you trying to get me drunk? Remember our agreement—that I'm not going to bed with you tonight!"

If he continues to make physical overtures to you and you feel you are entering the first stages of a sexual assault, you will need to increase the strength of your language:

"I know what you're trying to do. It's called rape!"

"I want you to know that if you continue, I will report you to campus security and the police department."

"Are you prepared for the consequences of your actions?"

"Are you prepared to be branded as a rapist by me and the police?"

"Are you prepared for what will happen to you if you continue this assault?

"You will lose your standing at the University."

"You will be known as a rapist."

"You will not be able to get a decent job and there is every possibility that you will go to jail! Are you prepared for that? If so, then I'm warning you that I will fight you with all of my strength!"

"I will prosecute you to the fullest extent of the law."

"I will pursue you and inform everyone that I meet that you are a rapist, and even if the authorities decide not to prosecute you, I can assure you that I will ruin you, if it's the last thing I do. Ten years from now, when you think you have forgotten me, I will remember you, and just when you think you will never hear from me again, I will be on your doorstep to inform your wife and your children that you are a rapist!"

Tell him you have a venereal disease or AIDS. Act crazy or as if you are on drugs and having a hallucination. Fighting back mentally may work just as well as physical action. Such maneuvers may make you too much for him to deal with.

These words may be uncomfortable for you just because you are saying things during a date that you normally would not say. You may be uncomfortable simply because you are not used to being assertive with him. The language may seem extreme, but it is meant to protect you from an attacker. You may have to pull out all the stops and be more aggressive than you've ever imagined.

You may fear that such assertiveness will put your relationship at risk, simply because he may not be able to handle a woman whom he cannot manipulate and control. Face facts. You may lose him, but think of the alternatives. If this guy is thinking of or planning to rape you, anything you can do or say that changes his plans is a victory for you. If he is so intimidated by your assertiveness that he drops you like a hot potato, then do you really want him in your life?

Remember, there are no guarantees. Anything can and often does happen. While confrontational words will work with some rapists in some situations, they may make him more violent if his personality bristles at being confronted by a woman. As with all crime prevention maneuvers, you take your chances no matter what you do. If he starts to get more violent or abusive when you verbally confront him, back off. Listen to your inner guidance to know exactly what to do and how to avoid making the situation even more violent.

Physical Maneuvers

There is a difference in the amount of force that generally accompanies date rapes from stranger rapes. Stranger rapists are generally more violent. For the date rapist, the act of having sex is how he exerts his control, while the stranger rapist is more interested in controlling and gaining power over his victim than in having sex with her. This kind of rapist may resort to violence to exert his power over the woman and physically abuse her along with the actual rape.

Fifteen Maneuvers That May Work

The following physical maneuvers are those that many people think are effective in stopping an attacker:

1. Kick him in the shins.

2. Slap his face.

3. Scratch his face.

4. Pull his hair.

5. Pull his little finger back to break it.

6. Kick him in the groin.

7. Pretend to faint.

8. Urinate, defecate, or vomit on him or on yourself.

9. Run from him.

10. Scream, "Help!" "Police!" "Rape!" or, "Fire!" Most experts believe you will get more response if you yell, "Fire!"

11. Make a loud noise or use a noise device.

12. Step on his foot, especially his instep, with your high heels.

13. Thumb to the eyeball push: When his guard is down, place your hands on each side of his face in a caressing motion. Move your hands toward the corners of his eyes and push your thumbs into the corners of his eyes. He will immediately go into shock, his eyes will pop out of his sockets and you should then have the opportunity to escape.

14. Testicle jerk: In this maneuver, you pretend to go along with the rape and get yourself into a position where you are close to his penis. Sooner or later, he will expose himself. Once he does, take hold of the testicles and jerk as hard as you can. This will cause him immense pain. He should bend over holding his crotch, which should give you enough time to escape.

15. If all of the above fail or are not possible, appear to cooperate. He is not expecting this and may then drop his guard or his weapon, giving you an opportunity to escape.

The date rapist is less likely to use excessive force on his victims. The physical maneuvers that most people associate with repelling a rapist will probably be more effective on the date rapist than on the stranger rapist.

Whatever is happening, try to remain calm if you can. Breathe deeply. This will reduce the shock and get oxygen to your brain which allows you to think more clearly. Keep your focus on distracting your attacker long enough for you to have an opportunity to escape.

Escape

Your primary objective is to escape your attacker. If you have an opportunity, you must take advantage of it instantly to get away from him. While you seek this opportunity, get as prepared as possible. If you are in high heels, get them off. You can't run in them. If you are not dressed for running, make whatever adjustments are necessary to get away. (Tight skirt? Get it up above your knees.) If it means that you have to run out of his place in your bare feet or partially clothed, don't hesitate. Move and move fast! Run toward light and people or get in a car and lock the doors and hit the horn until someone comes to your rescue. If you are in a parking garage or around a parked car, you can get down and crawl under the parked car—it will be hard for him to reach you there. (Scream "Fire" from under the car.)

Weapons

Many of the physical maneuvers listed above may not be effective during a stranger rape as there is generally less time to think. Stranger rapists are also more violence-prone and often use lethal weapons. These techniques are no match against a gun or knife.

Using some weapons yourself can be very effective in date rape situations because the date rapist is usually not armed and expects little to no resistance to his advances. It is important to be realistic, however, in choosing a weapon. Your boyfriend, father, or some other well-meaning man may quickly recommend carrying a gun, or even give you a gun. Think very carefully whether you can use it without hesitation in an assault situation. You may think you can, but many women faced with a criminal assault cannot effectively use a lethal weapon on an attacker, and end up hesitating. This hesitation may allow the criminal to gain control, confiscate the weapon, and use it against his intended victim.

Many women in this situation are in such a state of shock when their date/acquaintance starts to rape them that they do not interpret his actions as rape. This misidentification of a violent crime may cause additional delay in using a lethal weapon. The intended victim also may not understand that what is about to occur is a crime.

Susan Estrich writes in *Real Rape*, "It appears that most women forced to have sex by men they know see themselves as victims, but not as legitimate crime victims."

If a woman doesn't consider herself a "legitimate crime victim," how could she justify using force to stop the crime? Another reason she may not respond is that it is more difficult for some women to inflict pain on another person.

Most women are not taught as children to act aggressively towards other people. They tend to be more concerned about hurting another's feelings than men are. In fact some women are unfortunately more comfortable receiving pain than giving pain.

In many situations, a woman may find it so difficult to pull out the stops and injure her attacker, that she either hesitates or does not do it at all. She also may be worried that she cannot hurt him enough to stop him so she would rather not risk provoking him further.

Reality Check: Remember that there are NO guarantees. Anything you do or don't do could make the situation better or worse.

No one can give you absolute advice as to how to handle a rape situation. Every situation is different. Remember once again that what works for one woman, may not work for another. Every woman is different. Every rapist is different. Do what your inner guidance tells you to do.

Whatever you decided to do or not do, don't be too hard on yourself. Try not to blame yourself or judge yourself too harshly. Rape is a crime of violence and intimidation. If you escaped or survived, then you did exactly the right thing.

> **Reality Check: Whatever decision you made in the past, or make in the future, you did the best you could under the circumstances. Remember, if you make it through the assault alive, then you are not a victim. You are a survivor of a violent crime.**

You can come though this situation and recover. You do not have to face it all alone.

There are many people—doctors, police officers, lawyers, therapists, ministers, friends, family, and support groups—who can be of great help. Don't try and handle it alone. Don't try to ignore what happened to you and just continue your life as if nothing happened. You have had a life-threatening situation happen to you. You may suffer from post-traumatic stress disorder, just like a battlefield soldier, even if you escaped before the rape took place. Attempted rape can be extremely traumatic.

Find people who understand and care. Search the Internet. Consult the Yellow Pages. Talk to doctors, police, and therapists for referrals. Keep searching until you find the right therapist, support group, doctor, or minister, who knows what you're feeling and cares enough to help. Now that you are reading this book, you know there are many other women who have experienced what you have gone through.

You are not alone!

chapter ten

weapons, martial arts, and self-defense courses

No weapon or martial arts training is any good unless it's accessible and you are physically, mentally, and emotionally prepared to use it. Keep in mind as well that your weapon can be used against you. For this and other reasons, I strongly recommend against women relying on lethal weapons to protect themselves from rape. Non-lethal weapons are safer to use, but also can fail.

Here are the relative benefits and risks of both lethal and non-lethal weapons, and some caveats regarding martial arts and other self-defense training courses.

Guns

Thousands of people each year are killed in the United States because they own a gun they don't know how to use, or because it falls into the wrong hands.

Benefits: If you are extensively and/or professionally trained in firearm use, and you have a fair amount of experience with your weapon,

Before You Buy a Gun

Understand that you must take an approved safety course with a certified instructor.

You must commit to regular practice with the gun on a firing range.

You must commit to keeping any firearm clean and in good working order.

You should have a trigger-lock on it at all times, especially if you have any possibility of children around you or your house.

You must have a secure place that is locked up in which to keep it.

You must understand that no gun is any good to you if it is not accessible. In other words, it must be within reach when you are at home, in your car, on a date, or walking on the street. This may be impractical, if not illegal, since most states have laws prohibiting concealed weapons.

You will have to get a permit to carry a gun. You will not be allowed to carry it on public transportation, such as planes, trains, subways, and buses. You cannot carry it while attending sporting events, political meetings, or while in bars. There are many other restrictions pertaining to guns. Check your local laws before you make that purchase.

You must be physically, mentally, and emotionally prepared to instantly use a gun on another human being and take his life, and you must be prepared to accept the legal consequences of that action.

Guns kill and there is no going back once you have fired one. You must understand that hesitation also kills. The more you think, the longer you will tend to hesitate. The criminal will probably not hesitate in using his weapon. Can you do the same?

The right kind of gun should be appropriate for your size and personality. In most cases, it is ridiculous for a small woman to have a .357 magnum for protection.

you may be in a powerful position to protect yourself and others with it. If you are not extensively and/or professionally trained in gun use, a gun's benefits are dramatically outweighed by its risks. For most members of the general public, guns are not a good solution.

Risks: In addition to the always-present risk that your gun will be used against you, you must take on the responsibility and liability of gun ownership.

Knives

Second only to guns, knives are the most threatening and uncomfortable of all weapons. They are contact weapons and their effectiveness depends on the ability of the user to handle the weapon and not have it taken away. Since knives are contact weapons, you should understand that if you are close enough to use the knife on the attacker, then he is close enough to take it from you and use it on you. Knives are potentially lethal, depending on where you stab the attacker, but are rarely lethal on the first thrust. Usually, you would have to stab him over and over again to stop him. Knives, like guns, require the person using them to have made the decision to kill another human being in order for the lethal weapon to work.

Benefits: There aren't many. If you're trained in knife fighting and are prepared to get up close to your attacker, you can do significant damage to him.

Risks: Are you prepared to have a bloody knife fight with a potential rapist? Most women aren't. In most cases, you want to stay as far away from your attacker as possible. The mere thought of physically struggling with a rapist is so terrifying to women, that it makes the idea of carrying a knife for protection impractical. You also have to make sure that children do not have access to this weapon. There are laws regulating the length of the blade you can have on a knife.

Non-Lethal Weapons

I have taught crime prevention courses for a number of years to hundreds of thousands of people. My research indicates that the average person in most circumstances should not carry a gun or knife for protection. I strongly believe that there are devices available today that are effective, safe, and non-lethal. The greatest benefit of non-lethal weapons is that people will tend to use them without hesitation because they know that even if they make a mistake, no one dies. Still, not all of them are recommended.

Mace (CS or CN Tear Gas)

This non-lethal chemical was developed after World War II. Today, Mace comes in various sizes and shapes. They work by chemically stripping away the top layer of oil on the skin. This is done with acetone or some other strong astringent. When the oil is dissolved, the skin's nerve endings are exposed to the CS or CN chemical. This causes a painful, burning sensation, especially in the eyes. The effects last twenty to thirty minutes depending on the individual being sprayed, strength of chemical, and contact area. If you are attacked, spray the assailant in the face until the container is empty, then immediately escape. Following your escape, you must report the incident to the police.

Benefits: The product is inexpensive and does not require a training process to be able to use it. You just aim at the face and spray. If your attacker is a normal person with an average threshold for pain, Mace will do the trick. It will interrupt the assault long enough for you to escape. Mace is priced from $6 to $50 depending on size and has a range of three to twenty-five feet, depending on the unit and spray pattern. Shelf life is up to two years.

Risks: The attacker will, in many cases, not be stopped if he is under the influence of alcohol or drugs. These substances can raise the threshold for pain to such an extent that the attacker cannot feel the chemical. You also may have a problem if the rapist has thick and/or oily skin. Then the CS/CN tear gas may not be effective, since the thickness and level of oil in the skin may block the chemical. This chemical will not work at all on animals, because the fur and oil on the skin is so thick that the chemical never penetrates. Remember that this kind of non-lethal weapon works best in non-rainy, non-windy conditions, or when you are upwind from the assailant. This product should be replaced immediately upon its first use, since there is no way to tell how much you've used and how much is left in the canister.

Pepper Spray (Oleoresin Capsicum)

This chemical's properties are different from Mace, or CS and CN tear gas. Pepper spray basically was developed to be effective on all those people on whom Mace wouldn't work. Once the Capsicum (derived from the South American Chile Pepper plant) is inhaled into the assailant's nostrils, it restricts the breathing tubes, causing a choking sensation. The attacker will, in most cases, instinctively grab his throat and stop the attack. The pepper also will get into his eyes and they will not just burn, but will be slammed shut. The product has a two-year shelf-life and, like Mace, comes in various sizes and shapes. The chemical's strength is measured in Scovil Heat Units. The more heat it produces, the greater its effectiveness. I recommend the 10 percent strength. Remember, this kind of non-lethal weapon works best again in non-rainy, non-windy conditions, or when you are upwind from the assailant. Once again, after you spray the attacker, escape and report the crime to the police. The pricing is similar to CS and CN tear gas, $10 to $50.

Benefits: In addition to stopping assailants who are intoxicated or on drugs, it also can stop attackers who have a high threshold of pain since it works on the nostrils and lungs. It is also effective on animals. The National Park Service and many animal control personnel have been using

Pepper Spray for a number of years to control dogs, bears, and other animals. This chemical will work on almost all assailants, regardless of skin type, pigmentation, or level of oil on the skin. Its range is three to twenty-five feet, depending on the unit and spray pattern.

Reality Check: Remember, there are no guarantees with any product or plan of action.

Risks: Pepper Spray can and does work most of the time on most individuals. However, it does not work on everyone or every animal. There are cases where an assailant has been sprayed with a 10 percent Oleoresin Capsicum unit by several police officers, with no effects.

All chemical sprays are subject to bad manufacturing and leakage. The worst time to find out that your unit is not working is during an assault. You always should test the unit prior to using it in a criminal confrontation. With small "key-chain" sprayers, you can't practice with them or you will use them up. If you decide to carry Mace or Pepper Spray, you should carry a larger unit so that you can practice with it and you have more than one shot at the assailant. You also should be aware that with any chemical non-lethal device, there is a good chance that, during an assault, you will get sprayed as well. It's a good idea to prepare yourself for this possibility.

If you get sprayed, do not use any creams or salves and don't rub your eyes. Most chemicals can be washed off with water. In approximately thirty to forty-five minutes, the pain should dissipate and you should recover. It is wise to consult a doctor if you have an adverse reaction to the chemical.

Like guns, chemical sprays cannot be taken aboard airplanes, and some other modes of transportation. You cannot, in many states, carry them into an elementary or high school. You cannot carry them into court houses, government buildings, or other federal facilities. You should check with your local law enforcement agency to see what restrictions govern the carrying and use of chemical sprays.

A Word about Reporting the Crime: Why should you report the crime? If you don't, and the assailant reports you've used a weapon on him, you may find yourself arrested for assault. Law enforcement officials generally assume that, in the case of an altercation, the first person to report the incident is usually the victim. If you report it, you can explain the situation and why you responded as you did, even if it turns out that you over-reacted or sprayed an innocent person in error.

Stun Guns

Stun guns are not a gun at all but an electrical device similar to a cattle prod. They work by shocking the assailant with a bolt of electricity. The effectiveness depends on many things like voltage, climate, assailant's clothing, what part of the assailant's body you contact with the stun gun, and the charge of the battery. The part of electricity that stuns is the voltage, the part that kills is the amperage. Stun guns may have 50,000 to 150,000 volts, but very low amperage. Stun guns work by generating electrical charges that make the muscles constrict and expand rapidly. If the contact is in the right place on the body, the assailant's knees will buckle and he will fall down. This is a fairly expensive non-lethal weapon, ranging in price up to $150. Laws regarding stun guns are a little less restrictive, because it is a contact device and does not run the risk of contaminating a controlled environment's air system.

Benefits: There are few. Stun guns are best as a prevention tool. In other words, you can push the button and see a spark fly from one contact point to another and hear an electrical buzzing sound. At night, this display of electricity may ward off an attacker.

Risks: There are many. First of all, you must not only make contact with the assailant's side or upper leg, but you must maintain contact for up to seven seconds. This can be an eternity in a criminal confrontation. Remember, that if you're close enough to touch him, he is close enough to touch you. This product may or may not work if the attacker is wearing heavy clothes, such as a leather jacket, etc. Stun guns are battery-powered, using a nine-volt battery. The battery must be fully charged for the device to work adequately.

Tasers

Tasers are illegal in most areas. They are basically a stun gun with darts. Typically, they send out two darts with barbs on them. The barbs or darts are connected to wires that connect to the base unit, which you hold in your hand. Once the barbs are connected to the assailant, they complete the connection and send an electric shock. The range is about four to six feet, and, like stun guns, they are battery powered. The price range is approximately $50 to $150.

Benefits: The one benefit that a taser has is that, although it is a contact device, the contact generally is not close enough for the attacker to make contact with you. If he is four to six feet from you, you may be able to get away.

Risks: There are many. You only have one shot. If you don't connect with both darts, or the darts, due to heavy clothing, do not make contact with the assailant's skin, then the Taser may not work. There are no second shots, so you'd better make it count. Like stun guns, Tasers are vulnerable because they depend on a fully charged battery. However, the biggest risk is that they are illegal in most states and very unreliable.

Household Objects as Weapons

What follows is a partial list of the most common things around the house that people think of as potentially effective weapons against a rapist.

rat tail comb	hair spray	pens/pencils	oven cleaner
umbrella	rolling pin	hat pin	car keys
frying pan	purse/books	tire iron	fireplace tongs

Your goal is to incapacitate your attacker—you must put him on the ground long enough for you to escape. How long is long enough? About twenty to thirty minutes. This gives you enough time to clear the area. If he's on the ground for that amount of time, you have the time to get help or get to a safe area. Most of the common household items that you may have in your possession or close to you will not incapacitate the criminal, all they will do is hurt him. If you hurt him and don't hurt him enough to stop him, he will definitely hurt you!

Reality Check: In all cases, your only goal is to incapacitate him long enough for you to escape.

Weapons Can Fail

As with any man-made device, a weapon is subject to malfunctions and user error. There is no weapon that always works on everyone in all conditions. You take your chances with any lethal or non-lethal weapon. Don't think that just because you have a weapon, you can let your guard down. Your best weapon is your mind. Use it and trust your inner guidance to tell you what to do. There are no guarantees, whether you carry a weapon or not, whether you take a self-defense course or not, you still can be assaulted.

Martial Arts and Self-Defense Courses

Before you invest in a self-defense course, understand that there is a great difference between the fantasy of the martial arts movies and the reality of street combat. Assailants don't fight fair and will not pull their punches and abide by the classroom's rules. In a confrontation, everything happens very quickly. You should not realistically expect to become proficient in any martial arts discipline in a few short hours or weeks. This will take time and intensive commitment. What you may decide to do, as do many women, is to take a self-defense course, which can empower you with a few techniques and ideas to interrupt an assault long enough to escape.

Why Self-Defense Courses?

What is the difference between martial arts courses and self-defense courses?

There is a large distinction between the majority of martial arts and pure self-defense. Most martial arts offer long-term programs, often with many levels (belts) to be achieved, requiring the memorization of a series of choreographed techniques, one-step techniques, controlled sparring, the study of various weapons, etc.

Most women seek information on how to stay safe and/or fight back, and are not interested in spending four to six years studying a martial art in order to feel more secure. Self-defense is a conscious, proactive, methodical approach to life. It is comprised of a series of both learned and intrinsic behavioral and cognitive options that you must choose to put to work for you. And it may include a series of physical self-defense options which could be used, as a last resort, if you were to be physically attacked.

What can I learn?

A good self-defense course can provide many benefits. The following are some important areas that should be covered:

- Facts and statistics about crime and self-defense.
- Myths that keep violence against women in place and growing.
- Cognitive and behavioral options—tools like awareness and intuition that can be used to avoid violent crime.
- Boundary-setting information—how to communicate "No!"
- Physical self-defense techniques that an average person can learn easily, practice, and use if necessary. Courses that use padded male attackers, when presented safely and consciously, offer the most "real life" training experience.
- Information resources—survivor information and safety tips.

Where do I start?

If you're looking for a good self-defense course in your area and you're not sure where to start, here are some ideas on where to turn:

friends and relatives, rape crisis centers, private therapists and counselors, local colleges and universities, local Ys, fitness centers, your
state network against sexual assault, local law enforcement agencies,
local martial arts schools (some martial arts schools offer self-defense
seminars separately from the regular curriculum.)

What questions should I ask?

• Who is the instructor? Is the instructor male or female?

• What does the course teach? Does it offer a well-rounded curriculum with both physical and behavioral options?

• Will I have to "re-live" or "re-create" an attack if I have experienced one in the past? (If you have survived a sexual or other assault,
you may not want to re-live it in front of a class. Select a teacher who
does not require you to do that if you don't want to. However, learning how to fight and being able to practice on a padded attacker is
enormously empowering for a lot of people.)

• Is the course appropriate for my age group and level of previous
experience or skill?

• Where, when, how much and how long is the course?

(This information comes from The National Coalition Against Sexual Assault
website's guidelines for selecting a self-defense course by Kerry Kolmar,
Director of Martial Hearts, Inc.)

As with any choice in life, there is much to be said for listening to
your intuitive feelings. If it feels right to you, go with it. But do a little
homework before you decide on a course. Make sure it's the right time,
mentally and emotionally, for you to take this step.

Remember, there are no guarantees. You still can be victimized
even if you have taken a self-defense course or mastered a martial arts discipline. Once you've completed a self-defense course or become practiced
in martial arts training, it's up to you to put the information you gained to
work for you in your day-to-day life.

Realize that if you are attacked after having completed one of these courses, your ability to effectively use the physical self-defense options that you learned will be dependent upon your ability to remember what you learned in the course and your willingness to practice—with intensity and regularity—those techniques.

Use creative visualization—imagine getting attacked in a variety of environments and then see yourself using what you learned to defeat your attacker and emerge successfully from the situation. For more detailed information, see the National Coalition Against Sexual Assault website at www.ncasa.org/.

section two

surviving and recovering from sexual assault

chapter eleven

after the assault

If you have been raped or have experienced an attempted rape, you are not alone and you do not need to suffer alone.

Your immediate goal after the assault is to get to safety as quickly as possible. Your long-term goals are to recover physically, mentally, and emotionally, and to take back control of your body and your life so you can forge a stronger identity as a result of what has happened.

Whether you decided to fight with all of your strength, put up some resistance, or not fight back at all, you did not ask or deserve to be violated. Even if the rapist was not successful in completing his assault on you, you have been violated. You may tend to judge yourself for your actions or lack of actions during the assault, but no one, no matter what she has done, deserves to be raped. After the assault, be gentle on yourself. It was not your fault, no matter what you did or did not do.

Ten Things You Must (or Must Not) Do if You Have Been Raped

1. Get away from the rapist and get to safety.
2. Do not shower, bathe, douche, wash your hands, brush your teeth, or use the toilet. (If you do, you will destroy evidence of the assault.)
3. Do not change your clothing. (Again, this may destroy evidence.)
4. Do not straighten up your house or apartment if it was the scene of the crime. (Difficult as it may be not to, you may destroy important evidence if you do.)
5. Report the crime. (Call the police and campus security.)
6. Get a medical evidentiary exam. (Call your doctor, your health service, the local hospital, or a crisis center to find out where to go.)
7. Call someone whom you trust to be with you. (This person can make phone calls for you and accompany you to the police station or hospital. You may wish to have this person stay overnight with you.)
8. Contact a rape crisis center. (They will provide you with a great deal of information, as well as understanding and support.)
9. Get into counseling. (Find a good therapist, support group, etc.)
10. Be gentle on yourself. (Rape is a violent, life-threatening crime. Recovery takes time.)

Reasons to Report the Assault

Many women do not seek help for various reasons. Among them are their fears that the system will not be sensitive to their needs. They may not be aware of the resources in their area or they may want to minimize the severity of the crime. In date rape situations, there may be additional reasons that have to do with the relationship of the victim to the rapist, the status or connections of the rapist, or else the criminal is so popular or well-known that the victim feels no one would believe her. Knowing what to expect when you report the crime can diffuse your fears of the unknown.

There are countless reasons why you should report the assault:

• Police can help you get to a safe place and get a medical examination.

• Reporting the crime can help the police keep the rapist from attacking other women in the future.

• It is your right and responsibility. The only reason there are so many rape crisis centers and public support groups for victims is because women like yourself had the courage to come forward and report an assault regardless of the circumstances and/or consequences.

• Colleges are more likely to take actions to stop date rape if they are convinced there is a problem. Reporting the rape makes them aware.

• Reporting the assault will get you in touch with rape crisis and counseling centers, which you need to contact as soon as possible after the crime in order to recover as fully and rapidly as possible.

• You may be entitled to compensation. Many states have instituted victim compensation laws in which crime victims can apply for monetary awards from the state to pay for medical exams and physical therapy.

• Reporting the crime immediately after it occurs will help your credibility. However, even if you do not file a report, it does not mean the crime did not occur.

• Some rapists attack their victims again and will not stop their assaults until the police get involved. Sometimes, a rapist will end the assault with a threat that if you report the crime, he will come back and hurt you. Even if you comply, he may still harm you, and your compliance may cause him to think he can victimize you and get away with it. Reporting the assault, however, sends him a message that he cannot intimidate you and puts you back in control. Police intervention may be your best protection.

• Reporting the crime does not mean that you necessarily have to prosecute the attacker, but if you report it, you keep your options open in case you decide to prosecute at a later date.

• Keeping silent can hurt you psychologically and emotionally, and may inhibit your ability to get beyond the trauma.

• Rape crisis counselors, friends, family, etc., cannot help you unless they know about the incident. There are people out there who have been in your place and can help you get beyond this. You are not alone.

Reality Check: You have a choice to make—to do what is best for the rapist or to do what is best for *you!*

Following are some of the things you can expect when you report the rape to the police. These procedures are taken from *Recovering from Rape* by Linda E. Ledray, R.N., Ph.D., and from *Surviving Sexual Assault* by the Los Angeles Commission on Assaults Against Women. The individual procedures in your area may differ. The crime must be reported in the jurisdiction where the assault occurred. You may not be aware that many communities have psychologically trained investigative units that specialize in rape cases. These people have your interests at heart and will be sensitive to your feelings. (Please note that these units are more likely to be found in large metropolitan areas.)

Dealing with the Police and the Courts

Rape and attempted rape are both crimes, and as such will involve the police and the court system. The following information is not meant to overwhelm you with the legal process or scare you into not reporting the crime or prosecuting the rapist, but to let you know what will happen so that you can be prepared to handle it.

The Police

Call the general police phone number in your local telephone directory to verify jurisdiction of the precinct where the crime occurred. If you are unable to call, have someon call for you. It may be easier for you if you have a supportive friend with you. Your first inclination may be to call your boyfriend, lover, brother, or parents to go to the police station with you. If they are totally supportive and can handle it, they can be enormously helpful to you. However, many victims of rape find their families' embarrassment, fear, anger, and guilt may cause them to behave in unexpected ways. Choose a friend or a rape crisis counselor who will not judge you.

The police probably will ask you to come to the police station to file a report. If you are unable for physical or emotional reasons to go to the station, they may send officers to you wherever you are.

In filing a crime report with the police, you will be asked:

• Your name, address, place of employment, phone number, date, time, and location of the assault; and a description of the assailant.

• The details of the assault. This may be difficult for you, but they need to know. What happened? What did he do to you? What did he say to you? Try to be as accurate as possible and try to recall his exact words. Something he said may seem insignificant, but the police may be able to connect him to other assaults through his words or actions. The accuracy of your statements also will help your case during prosecution.

• Your activities before and after the attack. This may seem unnecessary, but again something about your activities before or after might become a clue as to why you were singled out.

• If you were drinking or using drugs. It is better to include this information in your report now. The detectives are not there to arrest you for your conduct—they are investigating a rape. Besides, if you do not include it now and decide to prosecute later, the rapist's defense attorney may discover it and use this information to discredit your testimony.

You may be in such a state of shock that it is difficult for you to tell your story. If you would feel more comfortable dealing with a female officer, ask for one. If you were raped or assaulted by a stranger, you may be asked to look at mug-shots and assist in making a composite picture. Do not be too hard on yourself if you cannot remember what he looks like. You have just come through a life-threatening situation. You may be in shock. Be patient, as your memory may come back to you later.

You also might be asked to identify a suspect in a lineup. This is generally done through a one-way glass or a specially lit room so that the suspect cannot see you.

After you make your report, you have the right to police transportation to your home. (If the assault occurred at your home or apartment, you may wish to be taken to another place.)

> **Reality Check: The police are not there to judge you. If any of their questions seem improper or accusatory, you have the right to ask why this information is necessary. You did not commit the assault—the rapist did. If the police seem to forget this fact, remind them that you or your actions are not on trial here.**

If you do not hear from the police in one or two days, you have the right to call and ask to whom the case has been assigned, and about the current status of the investigation. Keep in touch with those assigned to your case. If you think of any information that was not included in your report, do not hesitate to call to have it included. Everything is important!

You also may be interviewed by the prosecutor's office, and have to tell your story again. The prosecutor will decide whether there is sufficient admissible evidence to issue a formal complaint. Even if the state decides not to prosecute, that does not mean that the assault did not happen. It may only mean that there is insufficient evidence to gain a conviction.

The Criminal Courts

If the state does decide to prosecute, the suspect will be arraigned before a judge. You may or may not be required to attend.

If the suspect pleads not guilty, a hearing is set and you may be subpoenaed to testify at this hearing. It should take place within ten days (customarily within seventy-two hours) after the suspect is arrested, but delays are common.

If the judge presiding at the arraignment decides there is enough evidence, the case will go to trial. The suspect may be arraigned in court or, if he pleads guilty, the suspect will be charged and sentenced. You may not have to attend the pretrial hearing.

Your presence is required at the actual trial. The prosecuting attorney does not represent you; he/she represents the state because the defendant has broken the laws of the state. The prosecution is hired by the state, not by you. However, you are the star witness for the prosecution.

If convicted, the rapist is sentenced. If he is acquitted (due to lack of evidence), it does not mean you were not raped. It only means that the state could not prove its case beyond a reasonable doubt.

A trial can be a long and drawn-out process. You will need all the support you can get before, during, and after the trial. Get in touch with the rape crisis center and the victim assistance program in your area. They can help you understand what is happening in court and they may be able to help you with transportation to and from court if you need it. Get counseling or get into a survivors' support group. The local rape crisis center can give you information on the groups in your area.

The Civil Courts

You may wish to sue the rapist for damages. This is a civil suit and requires the services of an attorney, for which you will have to pay. This attorney, unlike the District Attorney, represents you and not the state.

Even if the assailant has no funds to pay you after a judgment is obtained against him, he is identified and embarrassed as a rapist. State laws may differ, but a judgment against him may interfere with his ability to buy or own certain property until the judgment is satisfied.

It is important to understand that the requirements (evidence and degree of proof) are not the same in a civil suit as they are in a criminal proceeding. Even if you lose the criminal case against him, you may win monetary damages from him in a civil court. Note that in a civil proceeding, you may be required to testify as to your sexual history. This generally will not be asked of you in a criminal proceeding.

The Medical and Evidentiary Exams

The following information will tell you not only what will happen during the medical examination process but also what your rights are. Even if you were able to escape before being raped, it is advisable for you to seek medical attention. There are four reasons why you need to get a medical exam immediately after the assault:

1. To calculate the extent of your injuries. It is common for the victim of a rape or attempted rape to go into a state of shock and numbness in which she will not realize the extent of her injuries.

2. To collect medical evidence for possible future prosecution. This evidence must be gathered as soon as possible. If you can be tested within twelve hours of the rape, there is a 95 percent chance the test for sperm and semen will be accurate.[14] The longer you wait, the more difficult it will be for the doctors to obtain usable specimens.

3. To settle fears you may have about AIDS or venereal disease.

4. To be tested for pre-existing pregnancy.

It is a good idea for you to call a supportive friend to come with you or meet you at the hospital. Have your friend bring an extra set of clothes for you as your present clothes may be taken from you to be used as evidence of the assault. You may want to have a female friend meet you as she may be more supportive than a boyfriend or family member right now.

Where do you go to get the examination? If you decide to report the rape to the police, they will know which hospitals have the services that you need. They also can put you in touch with a rape crisis center for counseling. If you decide not to report it, you can call your doctor for advice as to where to go.

Once you know which hospital to use, you should go to the emergency room, where, unfortunately, you may not be a high priority, especially if you have no outward signs of physical injury. This may mean that you will have to wait until the emergency staff is available to help you. The emergency room may not be warm, comfortable, or at all pleasant for you, especially at this time. In fact, it will probably be bright, cold, and impersonal. Be prepared for this—don't let it keep you from seeking medical attention. Any hospital that deals with sexual assaults should have a sensitively trained team of doctors, nurses, and psychologists who will help you through the process. Just in case you encounter impersonal or insensitive hospital staff, it is important to have a supportive friend accompany and help you during this exam.

During a medical exam:

• You may wish to call your personal physician to be with you during this procedure.

• Insist on being treated with gentleness and sensitivity.

• You can request privacy during the collection of medical evidence. If you are a minor, your right to have the exam take place without parents or guardians present will depend on local laws.

• You may request that police officers leave the examination room during the actual exam.

• You may request that a friend, family member, or rape crisis counselor be present during the exam.

• You have the right to have each procedure explained in detail before you allow the doctors to continue with the exam. Make sure you understand what the doctors and nurses are telling you. If you cannot decipher the medical terminology, ask them to stop and explain it to you.

The evidentiary exam is an examination for the purpose of obtaining evidence of sexual assault. It may include a pelvic exam. If forced sodomy or forced oral sex was performed, additional exams may be required of other parts of your body.

The evidentiary exam will document evidence of recent sexual intercourse, signs of force, and anything that could identify and incriminate the assailant.

Evidence of Recent Sexual Intercourse

The proof of recent sexual intercourse will be obtained by a collection of seminal fluids, sperm, vaginal secretions, and secretions from any other bodily areas involved in the rape, and samples of pubic hair. The absence of sperm does not mean that intercourse did not occur—many rapists are sexually dysfunctional, at least during the rape, and do not ejaculate during the assault.

Evidence of Force

It is important that evidence be obtained to establish proof that you did not consent to sexual intercourse with the rapist. The following steps may be taken:

Photographs may be taken of any bruises, abrasions, or injuries. Since bruises often do not appear for twenty-four to forty-eight hours, you may wish to request that the police take a second set of pictures at a later date when they become visible. (These pictures are useless as evidence if you take them yourself.)

Torn or soiled clothing worn during the rape will be held by the police for evidence. If you want it back, you will need to ask for it. Lack of physical signs of force does not mean that force was not used. Date rapists often use minimal physical force but *will* use extreme emotional and mental intimidation, which can have the same paralyzing effect on the victim as actual violence.

Blood samples may be taken to ascertain whether drugs and/or alcohol are in your system. This is likely if you indicate that you've used drugs or if you believe you have been drugged by the assailant. This evidence can show that you were not in control of your faculties at the time of the rape.

Exam Questions

The doctors and/or medical personnel may require a urine sample for pregnancy testing and may ask the following questions prior to the evidentiary exam:

What is your medical history?

What is your marital status?

What was the date of your last period?

Is your menstrual cycle regular?

Are you currently using birth control?

Have you ever been pregnant? If so, did you have a live birth, miscarriage, or abortion?

What was the date of your last sexual intercourse prior to the assault?

What is your recent sexual history?

Was the attacker using a condom?

You may find some of these questions personal and private, but understand that procedures and testing depend upon your answers.

Incriminating Evidence

This physical evidence is needed to build a case against the rapist. It may start to disintegrate with the passage of time. Some of the physical evidence also may disintegrate because of the weather. If you were raped outside, there may be physical signs of the attack that will be destroyed if it rains. This is another reason to report the assault as soon as possible.

A collection of the following may be taken to help build the State's case against the assailant: seminal fluids to determine the rapist's blood type; foreign matter still on your body such as leaves, fibers, hairs, etc., that will be used to identify your attacker.

After the evidentiary exam, you may wish to request copies of all medical reports. The victim assistance program in your area may be able to reimburse you for the expenses of your exams. You may request help in filling out the necessary forms to qualify for financial assistance. You have the right to strict medical confidentiality.

Pregnancy Testing

A urine specimen will be taken to determine if you were pregnant before the rape. You should be tested again to determine if you have become pregnant as a result of the rape. Some states will pay for this follow-up exam as part of the evidentiary exam if you have reported the rape within thirty-six hours of the assault.

If you do become pregnant, continue to seek advice from the rape crisis center and other qualified professionals who will continue to support you after you make a decision about your pregnancy. Your rape crisis counselor can do much to help you get into support groups whatever your decision may be.

chapter twelve

physical and emotional recovery

W hether you decided to fight or not, giving in to a rapist is not shameful. Rape is a violent crime. It is life-threatening. Getting on with your life is your utmost concern. Remember, you can heal only if you are alive!

Rape and sexual assault are trauma that may interrupt your life at home, work, or school, affecting your relationships with friends, family, and co-workers.

Although the process of recovery is often slow and confusing, with understanding and persistence you can accomplish a great deal. You have control over how you recover. The reassurance and support of friends, family, or your significant other is very important during this time, but their reaction to your experience may not be what you anticipate or would like it to be. People in your life will react in different ways—some may express blame, others may give you their full support. If you feel ready, you should allow those who offer their support to help you through this period—it will aid you in your recovery process. The decision to talk about your experience is a personal choice. You do not have to share your experience with anyone until you feel ready.

What You Deserve as a Survivor

You have survived an attack on your life. During the possibly chaotic aftermath of your experience, you may find yourself having to stick up for yourself and be your own advocate. Even though it is likely that your self-esteem has suffered as a result of your experience, keep in mind that you deserve nothing less than supportive, loving, caring treatment from everyone you encounter. Anyone who does not treat you well should be reminded of this. You deserve:

- to be believed.
- to be given the same credibility as any other crime victim.
- to seek help.
- courteous, efficient treatment.
- to be treated with dignity and respect, without prejudice against race, class, lifestyle, age, sex, or occupation.
- accurate information, presented in a way that you understand.
- to have your questions answered.
- to make your own decisions.
- to get help and support from others.
- to heal fully and completely and to take all the time you need to do so.

Your Individual Response

Your response to the assault can cover a wide range of physical and emotional symptoms, even some that may not seem to result directly from the attack. When you learn to recognize these symptoms, it will help you to gain control of them. Not every victim experiences all of these responses, and the following list only suggests several possibilities. You may experience these symptoms immediately, or months—maybe even years later—or you may never experience any of them. It all depends on each individual and the support you get from the people around you.

Common Emotional Reactions to Sexual Assault

Emotional Shock: Feeling numb, can't cry.

Disbelief: Questioning the event—Why me?

Embarrassment: What will people think?

Shame: Feeling dirty.

Guilt: It is my fault. If only I had…, etc.

Depression: Feeling tired and hopeless.

Powerlessness: Feeling out of control.

Disorientation: Feeling overwhelmed; can't sit still.

Re-triggering: Having flashbacks of assault.

Denial: Minimizing the impact of the experience.

Fear: Having nightmares; fearing pregnancy, AIDS, sexually transmitted diseases, intimacy; fearing you are going crazy.

Anxiety: Having trouble breathing; experiencing muscle tension; having difficulty sleeping; experiencing loss of appetite, nausea, stomach problems, nightmares, or bedwetting.

Anger: Wanting to get even. Wanting to kill the attacker.

Emotional Response

Rape survivors react in different ways after they have been raped, depending on many factors. There is no normal or abnormal, good or bad, right or wrong response to being sexually assaulted. A woman's reactions may depend upon her sense of self-worth before the assault, the extent of her relationship with the attacker, and the resources available to her after the attack. Her family dynamics (whether she will be blamed or shunned for being raped) and the amount of sincere support and caring her friends show after the rape also will affect the healing process greatly.

In the book *Recovering from Rape,* Linda E. Ledray, R.N., Ph.D., indicates some of the stages a rape survivor might face. The following reactions may occur in any order and be experienced at different intervals. You may stay in one stage for a long time, or you may skip one or more stages entirely. If you feel stuck in a particular stage for a long time, your counselor, therapist, or support group may be able to help you.

Emotional Shock and Disbelief—"Why Me?"

You may believe that rape cannot happen to good girls or that a rapist cannot possibly be a guy you know. If you believe the male-created myths that women who are raped wanted, provoked, or deserved the attack, you may be in shock and it may be more difficult for you to believe that the rape actually happened to you. You may feel numb and unable to cry. You may block out the rape and find it difficult to remember anything but the time before or after the rape. As you begin to get stronger and more emotionally able to deal with the assault, flashbacks and nightmares may occur. You also may feel weak, have trouble sleeping, and feel exhausted.

Embarrassment, Shame, Guilt

"I'm ashamed to tell anyone." "I can't tell my parents; they'd think I made it up." These are some of the things women say when they are feeling shame, guilt, or embarrassment about a date rape situation. Feeling embarrassed about being raped is a form of taking responsibility for the man's behavior. Women have not only suffered from rape and other forms of sexual assault, but they also have been ostracized by family and community for being victims. Your husband, boyfriend, family, or friends may not understand. Find someone who does. There is nothing for you to be ashamed of. *You* are not the rapist. He is the one who should be ashamed!

Disorientation

You may feel disoriented and confused by all that has happened to you as well as being inundated by the demands being put upon you at this time.

There are important decisions that have to be made, and even though you are in no emotional condition to think rationally, you still have to make them. This is another reason to contact a rape crisis counselor and/or support group who can empathize with what you are going through. You are not alone.

Anger, Rage, Revenge Fantasies

It is perfectly acceptable and normal to be angry with your attacker. In fact, it can be very healthy to be angry, because anger can become a moti vating force out of the feelings of helplessness, powerlessness, and worthlessness. Often, the feelings of anger and rage do not come until later, which is unfortunate because it can be easier to make decisions about your welfare if you have the energy of anger. You also may have thoughts and fantasies of elaborate revenge. Do not be too concerned about these feelings and fantasies—they are natural.

Depression

During the few days after the assault, you may experience depression. The severity of the feelings after the rape may be confusing to you, especially if you are being told by other people, "You're OK, just forget about it," or, "You're not hurt so what's the big deal?"

On an unconscious level, the impulse of family members and friends, even though they love you and have the best intentions in mind, is to minimize what has happened to you. This is a defense mechanism that enables them to deal with guilt they may be feeling for not having been able to protect you.

A common reaction to surviving a life-threatening situation is to become depressed. Depression may cause you to feel the following:

Discouraged about the future.

Feeling that you have nothing to live for or that things are hopeless.

Seeing only your faults exaggerated and the worst side of yourself.

Depression can be self-perpetuating and can last for an extended period, especially after the trauma of rape. Depression should not be ignored, as it is treatable and may get worse if not addressed.

Fear

When a woman is raped or sexually assaulted, she may fear the rapist and anyone who resembles him. In a date rape situation, a woman's trust of familiar men can be destroyed, leading to a total lack of trust in any and all men. She may lump all men together as potential rapists. Even boyfriends, lovers, and husbands are not immune to being considered in the same category as the rapist. It may be difficult for her to trust men. She may distrust her ability to differentiate a good (safe) man from a bad (dangerous) man.

Re-triggering

This is when something or someone reminds you of the rape. Often on the one-year anniversary of the assault, the survivor will have an emotional reaction. This also can happen if the rape occurred in a particular place like a parking garage in which case any parking garage could trigger an emotional reaction, because it reminds the woman of where she was raped. In date rape, this can be exacerbated because the rapist is often in contact with the victim after the rape. The trauma may be so great because of continual re-triggering incidents, that the victim might leave her job or school, or move away, just to stop the memories from recurring.

Other Physical and Emotional Reactions

You may become more dependent on friends and family or you may feel compelled to withdraw from people. It is common to have low self-esteem and to want to change your appearance so as to repel anyone who might be interested in you sexually.

Along with or as a result of the emotional responses, a sexual assault survivor may experience a wide range of physical responses, including: muscle tension, pain, shortness of breath, gynecological disturbances, fatigue, and changes in sleeping and eating patterns.

Feelings of despair may be temporary and pass quickly, however, when a life-threatening crisis like rape occurs, everything is serious and nothing should be taken for granted. If thoughts of suicide or self-harm occur, realize that they are normal, but a rape crisis counselor or therapist should be consulted at once.

Sexual dysfunction and promiscuity can occur in the aftermath of rape. Sexual dysfunction usually occurs if the victim views sex as synonymous with rape. If promiscuity occurs after a rape, it can be the most difficult for friends and family to understand and often gives them an excuse to disbelieve the woman's story.

Many people have rigid expectations of the way a woman is supposed to behave after she has been raped, expecting her to act hysterical, sob, have shredded clothes and black and blue marks from fighting off the rapist. If her behavior is not consistent with these expectations, others may disbelieve her.

Some of her girlfriends may minimize the assault or appear to blame the victim because they feel threatened—if their friend was an innocent victim, then perhaps they could be too. It may be easier to blame their friend instead of the rapist. Her friends may feel safer if they believe she caused the attack or made it up. Even her friends and family may seem tired of talking about the incident. This is also a way of denying that what happened was important and worth remembering.

Many people—family, friends, pastors, husbands, and others—will often get fed up with a woman's inability to "forgive and forget" and get on with her life. Forgiveness, which is the ultimate healer, cannot be embraced until she has worked through all of her other feelings in connection with the assault. These include anger, rage, hatred, fear, depression, and helplessness. There are no easy answers to recovery from this devastating crime.

Post-Traumatic Stress Disorder

If you have experienced a sexual assault, you may be left with painful wounds others can't see but that you know are there. Post-traumatic stress disorder (PTSD) can occur when normal people experience a terrifying situation they cannot control. In cases of sexual assault, PTSD symptoms can intrude into daily life and prevent a victim from working, having a relationship, or completing everyday tasks. If you feel this is happening, you may want to seek help. A counselor can help you identify and overcome PTSD.

Survivors with PTSD might encounter:
- Intrusive flashbacks, dreams, a need to dwell on the assault.
- Persistent or intense distress, anxiety, panic attacks, stress, sleep disturbance, irritability, fear, anger, apprehension, indecision, difficulty in concentrating, being easily startled, and sensitivity.
- Feelings of detachment or alienation.
- Persistent avoidance of people, places, and things associated with the assault.
- Ambivalence or uncertainties about the future.
- Avoidance of normal daily activity.
- Depression.
- Reliving the event as if it were still occurring.

What to Do to Help Yourself

You must take care of yourself physically and emotionally. The idea of seeing a doctor may seem unpleasant, but it is important for you to get medical attention. You don't have to go alone. Having a family member or

A survivor of sexual assault may experience any or all of the following:

Feeling dirty	Anxiety
Shock/numbness	Embarrassment
Loss of control over one's life	Relief
Fear	Grief
Sadness/depression	Loss of trust
Anger	Irritability
Suicidal thoughts	Denial
Preoccupation with safety	Guilt or self-blame
Shame	Apprehension
Indecision	Feeling stuck
Changes in perception of the world	

friend with you during the examination can help you feel at ease during the procedures. Your rape crisis counselor may be able to arrange for an advocate to accompany you.

Ask your medical professional to explain what he or she is doing before the examination, so that you know what to expect. Make sure your doctor understands your situation. You may be more sensitive than the average patient and may need more understanding, more time, or more reassurance during medical procedures, no matter how routine.

You can get treatment for your physical injuries and be tested for sexually transmitted diseases (STDs), including HIV, either at the hospital or by your private doctor. Early detection of STDs is very important. Discuss any medical concerns you have with your doctor or counselor, but don't let these concerns prevent you from receiving the medical treatment you need and deserve. Many rape survivors find that receiving medical attention helps them to regain a sense of control over their bodies.

Many rape survivors feel isolated in the aftermath of the assault. In order to reduce those feelings, reach out for support to those who are close to you: call family members, friends, or a rape crisis counselor. It might help you feel better to have someone to talk to, and you might want people around you for safety.

Consider professional support or counseling. Having someone to talk to about how you are feeling may help you to deal with the emotions you are experiencing because of the rape. Additionally, a counselor can help you build your relationships, express your needs to others, and get those needs met.

Give yourself some time off. You need time to recuperate. You may tend to want to forget what happened to you and get back to work or school as if nothing happened. This is denial and eventually only will inhibit or prolong your emotional healing. Sooner or later, the trauma will surface consciously or unconsciously and keep surfacing until you take the time and energy to deal with it. Just as with a physical injury to the body, you need time to heal. The mind and heart need time to heal as well. Just because you cannot see the emotional injuries doesn't mean they have not occurred and that you're healed.

Start your healing process by realizing you have choices as to how you react and how you view the assault. Keep repeating that it was not your fault. The tidal wave of feelings that may be happening to you now does not have to incapacitate you, if you realize that in order to get a handle on your feelings you must begin working with the way you think. Thoughts about the attack and the attacker may continue to pop into your head from time to time, but recognize that it is up to you to decide to what extent they will immobilize you.

There are many techniques and resources that will support you in your journey to healing. I have personally witnessed the effectiveness of affirmations, prayer, and other body/mind/spirit approaches. The "Suggested Reading" section of this book contains some of my recommendations for books, tapes, and videos. Visit a women's bookstore or a health food store to find more resources.

Individual and Group Counseling

Sexual assault can change your feelings about yourself and those around you. You may not feel the way you did before the assault—physically, emotionally, socially, or sexually. Counseling can help you to deal with these issues and aid you in your recovery.

Victim services or rape crisis counselors will listen, clarify, support, and explore options with you. Individual counseling sessions with a supportive counselor can help you identify issues you would like to resolve surrounding the assault. Together, you will develop appropriate, attainable goals for yourself.

Group counseling will give you the opportunity to share your feelings with other victims, and although each person recovers at a different pace, group counseling provides an environment in which survivors can share their experiences along with their techniques for recovery. Many group members find inspiration and motivation listening to the stories of other victims, and get a unique kind of support for returning to the lives they led before the victimization.

Consider Your Legal Rights

One of the most important decisions you may struggle with is whether or not to report the crime to the police. You may report the crime and still decide not to prosecute. By reporting, you may become eligible for crime victim compensation that will pay for medical costs such as counseling.

Speak with a counselor or someone you trust to determine which decision would be best for you. Whether you decide to press charges or not, you deserve support. The following list may help you feel better about your experiences since the assault.

• Accept that many of your responses are normal even if they do not feel comfortable. Coping means different things to different people.

• Develop a routine that is comfortable and that has a positive outcome. Having a routine can be very stabilizing in the face of traumatic stress.

- Recognize that your assault will affect others around you.
- Develop strategies for gaining support and understanding. Different strategies will be effective with different people.
- Take care of your health. A regular diet can lead to well-being. Sugar and caffeine can increase your stress level.
- Alcohol and drugs may delay some reactions and ultimately make them worse. If you find you are abusing alcohol or drugs, you should contact a counselor immediately.
- Allow time for adequate amounts of rest and relaxation. Some techniques to consider are meditation, deep breathing, listening to music, reading, religious rituals, or anything that focuses and relaxes you.
- Physical activity is a great stress-reducer, even if it's just a short walk. Try to exercise every day.
- Supportive listeners can include friends, family, religious leaders, teachers, professional counselors, or counseling groups.
- Patience and understanding are important in the recovery process. It takes time. In addition to the support of friends, family, and loved ones, there are also professional counselors who can assist you.

Reality Check: Rape is a crime of power over another person. During the rape or attempted rape, the rapist takes your power away from you by force or intimidation. After the rape, take back your power.

Don't Give Up

Long after the physical body has healed from the assault, the emotional and mental healing will continue. Some experts and psychologists have indicated that the emotional impact of sexual assault can continue for years after the attack. Don't give up five minutes before the miracle. The emotional recovery from date/acquaintance rape often takes much longer than if it was a stranger rape situation. This is because there is an unspoken bond of trust that exists in every dating situation; this is destroyed in a date/acquaintance rape or even in an attempted date/acquaintance rape. This destruction of trust is very serious and substantially inhibits the normal healing process. When that trust has been violated, it takes longer for a woman to trust men whether she knows them or not. Most women are familiar with the possibility of assault from a stranger but not from men they know and trust. That is what makes date/acquaintance rape so insidious.

It is important to remember that *he* made a deliberate choice to take from you privacy, your sense of safety, your trust, and your control of your life and body. It was not your fault. He was perfectly able to stop. He simply chose not to, no matter what you said or did.

It's not your fault!

no matter how stupid you may feel,
no matter if you knew the guy,
no matter if you were high on drugs/alcohol,
no matter if you originally said, "yes," then said, "no,"
no matter if you've had sex with him before,
no matter if no one believes you,
no matter if you choose not to report it,
no matter what happened, it's not your fault!

The emotional roller coaster that happens after a date rape can last for years; however, the length of recovery can be reduced if you get professional help for yourself. It is natural to want to deny what has happened and get on with the rest of your life. However, the fears, anger, rage, panic attacks, feelings of worthlessness, and the occasional feeling that you may be going crazy cannot be buried or denied for long. Sooner or later, these feelings will surface and when they do, they may adversely affect your other relationships, especially with lovers, husbands, friends, or family. Your job and your ability to function also may be affected

Getting help from a qualified rape crisis counselor or therapist will help you deal with the complex and potentially self-destructive feelings that you may be going through. No one who has survived a rape or attempted rape deserves to be judged. What she needs, as do all rape survivors, is support, understanding, and help in her recovery.

Reality Check: Rape is one of the only crimes in which society tends to blame the victim.

Spiritual Healing

In this chapter, I have talked about mental and emotional healing, but there is another aspect of ourselves that I have not talked about. This is spiritual recovery.

Women who have been raped have been shunned by their families, friends, and husbands, and in some cultures, the prevalent belief is that the victim has "sinned against God" and was therefore being punished. No belief is as destructive to a woman's self-worth as this. If you are religious, you may be torturing yourself with these feelings. You can counteract these negative emotions by repeating the following statements to yourself:

I accept that I have been violated.

I accept that I am starting to cope with my feelings about the assault.

I accept the anger that I feel about my violation, but understand that my anger can be a temporary part of my recovery and I have control over whether it intrudes into my life in an inappropriate way.

I give myself permission to talk about my experience with a trusted counselor or therapist.

As I understand my feelings about the assault, I realize that I am on the road to recovery.

I can and do give the responsibility for the assault to the perpetrator of the crime.

I did the best that I could in preventing the assault, and I am determined to do the best I can in my recovery.

My self-esteem is increasing as I learn to value myself a little more each day.

I am learning to trust myself more each day and the choices that I make.

I am learning to accept what has happened to me and I am feeling more at ease each day.

I understand that it is my choice if and when I forgive my assailant.

Each day the assailant has less control over me as I learn to have greater control over myself.

Although I will never be the same person I was before the attack, I am healing, growing, and recovering, and I will make it through this process a stronger person.

Reality Check: There is no justification, either religious or otherwise, in believing that your rape is God's punishment.

Rape is not an act of God. It is an act of violence and intimidation against not only a woman's body, but also against her very soul, regardless of her religious upbringing or affiliation.

This time of recovery can be a time to reflect inward. Pray, meditate, ask for peace of mind and the help you need to heal.

What Friends and Family Can Do

Rape is a crime that has many victims—not only the actual person who was raped, but also friends, lovers, family, and anyone who is currently in a relationship with the victim or the rapist. The significant other's response to the survivor after the rape can be the most important factor in her healing. If you are involved with or related to a woman who has been raped, you may experience any or all of the following emotions:

Guilt: It is common for you to feel guilty for not being there to protect her.

Anger: Obviously, you will be angry at the rapist, but taking the law into your own hands and rushing out to get the guy is not what she needs right now. She has enough to worry about without wondering if you are going to get killed or put in jail. Your rage against the rapist may be interpreted by her as anger or violence against her as well.

Depression: You, like she, may get depressed at the incident because it has changed both of your lives forever. She may withdraw from you and seem to change. This is normal. You may want your relationship to go back to the way it was as quickly as possible. This is unrealistic and unfair. It also places blame upon her because she can't get beyond the incident according to your time table. Give her time!

Denial: You may react by pointing out that she did not get hurt, so why can't she just forget about it? This attempt to minimize her pain only will make her feel more isolated from you and the world, as well as tell her that you really do not understand what she is going through. She may really need to talk it through—let her.

Disbelief: You may not believe everything she tells you about the incident. Maybe she did not act the way you think she should have or maybe she was not physically beaten to the degree that there are bruises. If you do not believe her, it will only harm her. She needs your unconditional support right now. Do not hold back. If you have trouble understanding her, her story, and the way she's reacting to you, contact a rape crisis counselor who can give you some insight into her condition.

Over-protection: You may want to take control of her life, never leave her alone, etc. Remember, she has just gone through a situation in which her control was taken away from her. She needs to feel that you will protect her but also will encourage her to take control of her life again.

What She Needs from You

The journey from pain takes time and involves releasing fears. She can grow in spite of her pain if she gets support. Be patient with her moods, never give up on her, and accept her own unique way of dealing with her trauma. Ultimately, this experience can be used as a means to change her life for the better, depending on how she looks at it, but for now, allow her the time to heal without your time limits or your expectations. Give yourself time to heal as well. Be honest in your own needs and avoid denial, it only leads to emotional blocks.

You may need professional help in order to understand and cope with the aftermath of rape. Here is how you can best support your friend or loved one:

Believe her. Regardless of the circumstances, if she feels that she has been raped, then she has. Do not question her, even if her story does not make sense. She may be withholding details in order not to upset you. She has just been through a brush with death, and that is bound to have an effect on her.

Reassure her. She needs to know what she is feeling is normal for someone who has been raped. She is bound to have many confusing feelings right now. Tell her it's OK, that it's going to take time for her to recover. Express some of your own feelings as well. It will give her permission to share what she is feeling.

Listen to her. Hear what she is really saying about herself. Do not close the door on what has happened before she is ready. Every rape survivor responds differently to the assault and recovery time varies. Trying to minimize the attack's impact on her will isolate her and drive her away from you. Be patient.

Let her know how you feel. Share your feelings with her as well as with a rape crisis counselor or therapist. Don't tell her, "I understand," or, "I know how you feel," unless you have been victimized by rape yourself. You can't know how she feels. Just listen and be there for her.

Don't take control. It is normal to want to rescue her, to protect her, to surround her with your presence. Be patient. Reassure her that you will be there as much as she needs, but that you know she is capable of making decisions and being in control of her own life. Besides, you can't be there all the time for her. Her independence should always be encouraged.

Patience, patience, patience. Don't expect too much from her. Her ability to recover and the length of time it will take depends on you, her family, the kind of help she gets, and her self-esteem prior to the rape. Understand that if your sexual relationship changes, this is normal. She may take her anger out on you. On a subconscious or conscious level, she may put you in the same category as the rapist. She may feel that all men are the same. Keep telling her, "I'm on your side," and, "I know you're angry, I'm angry too." Encourage her to get professional help and agree to get help with her. Although you were not the one who was raped, you both need to deal with the stress of the rape on your relationship. In fact, you were both victimized by the rapist. There is nothing wrong with getting help for yourself with a therapist or a professional counselor.

section three

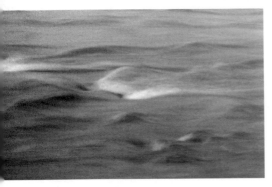

sexual assault: harassment, stalking, dating, & domestic violence

chapter thirteen

sexual
harassment

Date and acquaintance rape often starts as a series of intimidations and manipulations of a sexual nature. This is called sexual harassment, and it can be a confusing issue today, but you should understand that you can be harassed regardless of your age or appearance. Many women have experienced sexual harassment, and the law is beginning to address this area.

According to a *USA Today* report, "Although it can be a precursor to acts of violence and other criminal acts, sexual harassment is not itself legally classified as a crime in most jurisdictions in the U.S.; therefore, it can only be addressed through a civil action."[15]

Sexual harassment is unwanted, repeated sexual attention. It's not only offensive—it's against civil law. Sexual harassment is illegal even if the harasser is not your boss, your professor, or your teacher. It is illegal even if the perpetrator is not overtly stating to you that you will lose your job or your academic standing if you don't go along with his sexual contacts. It also is illegal if the harassment creates a hostile or offensive environment which interferes with your ability to do your job or continue your academic pursuits.

Here are some behaviors that the law may deem to be sexual harassment:
- Slurs or abuse
- Sexual innuendoes and other suggestive, offensive, or derogatory comments
- Humor and jokes about sex (or gender-specific traits)
- Sexist remarks about your body, clothing, or sexual activity
- Sexual propositions or subtle pressure for sexual activities
- Insults of a sexual nature
- Requests or demands for sexual favors
- Catcalls
- Leering, ogling, whistling
- Suggestive or insulting sounds or gestures
- Use of inappropriate body images to advertise events
- Visual displays of degrading sexual images
- Unnecessary and unwanted physical contact (e.g., touching, brushing, pinching)
- Attempts to impede or block movement
- Attempted or actual fondling or kissing
- Physical assault or coerced sexual intercourse

The basic point to remember is that sexual harassment is unwanted, unsolicited, or undesired attention of a sexual nature. Sexual harassment is a breach of the trusting relationship that normally exists between the employer and employee or the professor and student. Boundaries between the professional role and the personal relationship blur because of what the harasser introduces into what should be a sex-neutral situation. Sexual harassment can escalate into rape.

Reality Check: Sexual harassment is not about sex—it's about power. Typically, such behavior is designed to humiliate and control.

Both males and females can be victims of sexual harassment, and both males and females can be perpetrators of sexual harassment, although as with other types of sexual assault, the majority of harassment is perpetrated by men against women. More than half, and perhaps as many as two-thirds, of sexual harassment cases recorded by the Equal Employment Opportunity Commission involve male perpetrators and female victims.[16]

Hostile Environment

In a "hostile environment" claim, the complainant must demonstrate that a reasonable person would find the working environment hostile and abusive, and that she herself was offended, a requirement easily met where the offending conduct has affected psychological well-being in a demonstrable way. Even without serious psychological injury, the employee may still show that the conduct was offensive. If, however, she herself contributed by speech or actions to a sexually charged atmosphere, the employee may be unable to show that her complaint is legitimate.

In addition, not all conduct of a sexual nature in the workplace is unlawful. The touchstone of whether harassment has occurred is whether the challenged conduct is unwelcome. The courts have stated that an isolated comment will not constitute harassment. Rather, the totality of the circumstances must be considered, including the frequency and severity of the offending conduct, whether it is physically threatening or humiliating, and whether it unreasonably interferes with the employee's performance.

Current law does not require that a victim of sexual harassment first make an internal complaint before filing a claim. However, if the employer has a complaint procedure that encourages victims to come forward, failure to complain may undercut efforts to show that the employee was offended. If the employer has no complaint procedure, or if the procedure would require the victim to report the complaint to the harasser, then the lack of complaint won't affect the employee's case.

How to Prevent or Deal with Sexual Harassment

Sexual harassment is illegal and most corporate and school policies prohibit any employee or student from engaging in sexual harassment.

Speak up at the time of the perceived harassment situation: Say "No!" clearly, firmly, and without smiling. This is not the time to be polite or vague. Inform the harasser that his attentions are unwanted. Make clear that you find the behavior offensive. By being quiet, you enable the harassment to continue. Speaking up can protect others from being victimized and may decrease your feelings of helplessness. If you have clearly requested that the behavior stop and it doesn't, write a memo to the harasser and keep a copy in your files.

Document the harassment. Write down each incident including date, time, and place. Detail what happened and include your response. Keep a copy at home. This information will be useful if you need to take legal action.

Document your work. Keep copies of performance evaluations and memos that attest to the quality of your work. The harasser may question your job performance in order to justify his behavior.

Look for witnesses and other victims. You probably are not the first person who has been mistreated by this individual. Ask around—you may find others who will support your charge. Two accusations are much harder to ignore. Don't be too disappointed if you find other women who have been harassed but are willing to ignore it—these people may be afraid for their jobs or have become so used to the offensive behavior that it doesn't bother them anymore. Sexual harassment will continue if good people do nothing.

Explore university and company channels. Use any grievance procedures or channels detailed in your employee handbook. If you are in a union, get the union steward involved right away.

Seek advice. This can help you determine if what you are experiencing is sexual harassment and can provide help in preventing initial overtures from developing into harassment. You may begin by seeking advice from your human resources department, your union representative, your dean of students, or from an attorney or legal service. You do not need an attorney to file a sexual harassment claim, but before filing a claim, you may want to speak with a legal service or private attorney specializing in employment discrimination. For information on where to seek advice, call 9 to 5, an advocacy organization of working women. Several of their chapters have formed sexual harassment support groups. Their toll-free number is (800) 522-0925.

File a complaint. If you need to pursue a legal remedy, contact your state discrimination agency or the federal Equal Employment Opportunity Commission (look in your telephone directory for the field office closest to you. The federal agency covers workplaces of fifteen or more people. State law may protect you if you're in a smaller workplace).

Don't blame yourself. Sexual harassment is unwanted action that the harasser decides to take. It is not your fault.

Don't delay. If you delay action, the harassment is likely to continue.

**Reality Check: Victims of sexual harassment are entitled to
damages for pain and suffering as well as to any lost pay.
If you win, you may recover legal fees.**

If You Observe Sexual Harassment

If you are an observer of what you perceive to be sexual harassment, you can take steps to stop this form of discrimination. You can:

- Speak up. Inform the harasser that his/her actions may be perceived as sexual harassment.
- Support the victim. Provide comfort and assurances to the victim.
- Report the incident to appropriate persons within your office or school.

New Liability for Schools

Historically, if one student harassed another, the school itself could not be sued or held responsible. This appears to be changing. In a Georgia case brought before the U.S. Supreme Court in 1999, a young girl had been continually harassed in school and, despite her mother's complaints, the school had done nothing to assist her. The mother sued the school and the Court ruled that a school can be sued in civil court for not stopping one student from harassing another if the conduct has been reported to the school. This makes schools directly responsible to take action against sexual harassment between students, once the harassment is brought to the school's attention. This case has removed the immunity from lawsuits that schools have historically enjoyed, and left schools throughout the country scrambling to formulate policies and procedures to prevent and otherwise deal with sexual harassment issues.

chapter fourteen

stalking

Probably the most insidious of the sexual crimes is that of stalking—the never-ending control, manipulation, and pursuit of the intended victim. In general, it is such a heinous crime that the stalker rarely ends his pursuit until either he, or the victim, is dead.

Stalking is legally defined primarily by state statutes. While statutes vary, most define stalking as a course of conduct that places a person in fear for personal safety. The variety of specific strategies employed and behaviors displayed by stalkers are limited only by the creativity and ingenuity of the stalkers themselves. Suffice it to say, virtually any unwanted contact between a stalker and his victim which directly or indirectly communicates a threat or places the victim in fear can generally be referred to as stalking.

Stalking is not a new phenomenon. Until recently, it was not labeled as a separate and distinct class of deviant behavior, but referred to as harassment, annoyance, or, in some cases, simply as domestic violence. In the 1980s and 1990s, numerous high-profile cases involving celebrities began to catch the attention of the media and public policy leaders. Only then did such behavior begin to be described as "stalking." Since then, stalking has become a common subject in the popular media. With the advent of blockbuster films from that time period—such as *Fatal Attraction*, *Cape Fear*, and *Sleeping with the Enemy*—and its coverage by the news media, "stalking" has become a household word.

Until recently, law enforcement officials did not track the incidences of stalking offenses as part of their normal crime reporting process. Since there has been virtually no empirical data available, no one knows just how common stalking cases are in the United States.

Best estimates indicate that as many as one of every twelve American women (8.2 million) and one of every forty-five American men (2 million) has been stalked at some point in their lives.[17] Seventy-eight percent of stalking victims are female, whereas 87 percent of stalkers are male. The first anti-stalking law was passed in California in 1990. With the passage of the 1994 Crime Bill by the U.S. Congress mandating the tracking and compilation of stalking crime statistics, experts are beginning to determine more accurately the prevalence of this crime.

Fifty-three percent of stalking cases are reported to the police.

About 12 percent of all stalking cases result in criminal prosecution.

About a quarter of female stalking victims and about a tenth of male stalking victims obtain restraining orders against their stalkers.

Sixty-nine percent of women with restraining orders and 81 percent of men with such orders said their stalkers violated the order.

The Two Types of Stalkers

There are two types of stalkers, and both females and males can be victims or perpetrators. However, most stalkers are men, and male stalkers generally are more violent. Statistics indicate that 75 to 80 percent of all stalking cases involve men stalking women.[18] Most stalkers are in the young to middle-age range, have above-average intelligence, and may come from any cultural and socio-economic background.[19]

Unfortunately, there is no single psychological or behavioral profile for stalkers. In fact, many experts believe that every stalker is different, making it very difficult not only to categorize their behavior, but doubly difficult to devise effective strategies to cope with such behavior. Forensic psychologists, who study criminal behavior, are just beginning to examine the minds and motives of stalkers. These psychologists have identified two broad categories of stalkers and stalking behavior—"Love Obsession" and "Simple Obsession."

Love Obsession Stalkers

This category is characterized by stalkers who seem to develop a love obsession or fixation on another person with whom they have no personal relationship. The target may be only a casual acquaintance or even a complete stranger. This category represents about 20 to 25 percent of all stalking cases.

Those who stalk celebrities and stars—such as David Letterman, Jodie Foster, and Madonna—fall into the category of love obsessionists; however, stalkers in this category also include those who develop fixations on regular, ordinary people including co-workers, casual acquaintances, or people they pass in the street.

The vast majority of love obsession stalkers seem to suffer from a mental disorder—often schizophrenia or paranoia. Regardless of the specific disorder, nearly all display some delusional thought patterns and behaviors. Since most are unable to develop normal personal relationships through more conventional and socially acceptable means, they retreat to a life of fantasy relationships with persons they hardly know. They apparently invent fictional stories—complete with what is to them real-life scripts—which cast their unwilling victims in the lead role as their own love interest. They then attempt to act out their fictional plots in the real world.

The woman who has stalked talk-show host David Letterman for years seems to truly believe she is his wife. She has been discovered on Mr. Letterman's property numerous times, has been arrested driving his car and has appeared at his residence with her own child in tow—each time insisting that she is David Letterman's wife. Love obsessional stalkers not only attempt to live out their fantasies, but appear to expect their victims to play their assigned roles as well. They seem to believe they can make the object of their affection love them. They desperately want to establish a positive personal relationship with their victim. When the victim refuses to follow the script or doesn't respond as the stalker hopes, they may attempt to force the victim to comply by use of threats and intimidation. When threats and intimidation fail, some stalkers turn to violence. Some decide that if they cannot be a positive part of their victim's life, they will be part of their life in a negative way—sometimes even going so far as to murder their victims in a twisted attempt to romantically link themselves to their victim forever. This was the case with the man who shot and killed Rebecca Schaffer, the young actress and star of the 1980s television sit-com *My Sister Sam.*

Simple Obsession Stalker

This second category represents 70 to 80 percent of all stalking cases and is distinguished by the fact that some previous personal or romantic relationship existed between the stalker and the victim before the stalking behavior began. Virtually all domestic violence cases involving stalking fall under this umbrella, as do casual dating relationships (commonly referred to by law enforcement agents as "Fatal Attraction" cases, named after the popular movie by the same title).

While this kind of stalker may or may not have psychological disorders, all examined clearly have personality disorders. One forensic psychologist has attempted to identify some of the common personality traits and behavioral characteristics among this category of stalker. Stalkers in this class are characterized as individuals who are:

- socially maladjusted and inept;
- emotionally immature;
- often subject to feelings of powerlessness;
- unable to succeed in relationships by socially acceptable means;
- jealous, bordering on paranoid; and
- extremely insecure about themselves and suffering from low self-esteem.

The self-esteem of simple obsession stalkers often is tied closely to their relationship with their partner. In many cases, such stalkers bolster their own self-esteem by dominating and intimidating their mates. Since the victim literally becomes the stalker's primary source of self-esteem, his greatest fear becomes the loss of this person. The stalker's own self-worth is so closely tied to the victim that when he is deprived of that person, he may feel that his own life is without worth. This is what makes simple obsession stalkers so dangerous. In the most extreme cases, these stalkers will stop at nothing to regain their "lost possession"—their partner—and in so doing, regain their lost self-esteem.

Just as with most domestic violence cases, stalkers are the most dangerous when first deprived of their source of power and self-esteem— in other words, relationship. Indeed, stalking cases that emerge from domestic violence situations constitute the most common and potentially lethal class of stalking cases.

If you are attempting to break off a relationship with a simple obsession stalker, he will desperately connive ways to get the relationship

re-started. If you resist him or don't cooperate, he may use force or intimidation. If threats and intimidation fail, he may turn to violence. He
cannot be objective about his ex-partner. He has only one desire, and that
is to return to what he felt was the "perfect relationship." He may define
himself through that relationship and feel like a failure if the relationship
fails. His violence may escalate to homicide from an obsessive belief that
if he cannot have his victim in this life, then he will have her in the next.

Stalking Behavior Patterns

Stalking behavior patterns are in many ways similar to domestic
violence. Much of the behavior is initiated when the stalker's attempts
to control the victim are resisted. This happens during a relationship
breakup as well as in the initial stages of a new relationship. The stalker
may try to control his victim by sending flowers, candy, love letters,
or expensive gifts. If she doesn't cooperate and return his affection, he
may turn to intimidation. He may start by being jealous and wishing
to have control over everything she does and everyone she sees.

There are basically three steps or stages in a stalking situation. If you
recognize this behavior pattern in your life, either as a perpetrator or a
victim, you should seek professional help immediately.

The stalker's thoughts often progress from, "If I can just prove to you
how much I love you!" to, "I can make you love me!" to, "If I can't have
you, nobody else will!"

This progression in a stalker's thinking is common, however we cannot
as yet predict a stalker's behavior. Some stalkers may threaten and intimidate at any point. Every situation is different and there is no one way to
respond to a stalker's behavior that will prevent an escalation of violence.

Stalking and the Law

The first anti-stalking law was passed in California in 1990. In 1992, the U.S. Congress enacted legislation that required the Attorney General, through the National Institute of Justice, to conduct research on the issue of stalking and to develop and distribute among the states a "constitutional and enforceable" model anti-stalking code.[20]

As of September 1993, all fifty states and the District of Columbia had some form of anti-stalking law. In 1996, the U.S. Congress passed the first federal stalking law. Beyond a basic definition of the crime, statutes include a wide variety of additional stalking-related provisions. For example, some state stalking statutes:

- allow police to make arrests without a warrant in stalking cases where probable cause exists;
- make stalking a non-bailable offense under certain circumstances;
- provide for automatic and emergency protective orders;
- require mandatory psychological evaluation and treatment for stalkers;
- establish sentencing enhancements in cases where the victim is a minor, or when there is a protective order in place against the perpetrator;
- create heightened crime classifications for stalkers who commit multiple stalking offenses.

Until the anti-stalking legislation was enacted in most states, victims had few alternatives. Most laws in the past have not given adequate protection to victims of stalking because they were intended to prosecute the stalker after he had already committed the crime. Watching, following, and intimidating another person was rarely taken seriously until physical damage was committed. Traditionally, women were told that the only recourse they had was to take out a restraining order. These rarely had any effect because they are designed to control the behavior of rational individuals who do not wish to commit a crime and go to jail. In essence, they were designed for people who had respect for the court's authority.

A stalker is not coherent enough to understand or care about what the court orders and tends to be out of touch with reality.

For these reasons, legislators across the nation have implemented stalking legislation that protects individuals from stalkers. Anti-stalking legislation makes it a crime to engage in a pattern of behavior that harasses and/or threatens other people.

Three Types of Anti-Stalking Laws

Generally, anti-stalking laws can be classified into three different categories related to penalties:

1. those that make stalking a misdemeanor,
2. those that make a first offense of stalking a misdemeanor and subsequent offenses felonies, and
3. those that make stalking a felony.

For additional information about your state's anti-stalking laws, contact:

Your state Attorney General's office

Your local prosecutor's office or law enforcement agency

Your local law library, or the reference librarian in your local library

Statutes that establish new crimes, such as stalking, are not universally implemented or instantaneously enforced from the moment they take effect. There is often a considerable lag time in implementing new statutes as law enforcement officials, prosecutors, and judges become familiar with the law and develop policies and procedures to implement them.

Since stalking laws are fairly new, victims cannot always be certain that law enforcement officials, prosecutors, or even judges are aware of these new laws. Stalking victims may find it necessary to provide law enforcement officials with a copy of their state stalking statute, along with evidence which proves the stalker has violated the statute. Copies of such statutes can be found in your state's published criminal code, available in some public libraries and all law libraries.

Preventing and Dealing with Stalking

If you are a victim of stalking you must document all contact with the stalker, no matter how insignificant. The court will look at the conduct of the stalker and consider whether his behavior is reasonable or unreasonable. The court will take into consideration a victim's feelings and how much fear the stalker has caused through his actions. A complaint must be accompanied with sufficient evidence to establish "probable cause" that the stalker engaged in conduct that is illegal under the state's stalking statute. If law enforcement officials do not witness such conduct first-hand, it is often up to the victim to provide them with the evidence necessary to establish probable cause.

You must be familiar with your state's stalking law to know if your stalker is indeed breaking the law. In Georgia, for example, a stalker cannot be prosecuted if he is watching you from his own residence. For instance, if a man is stalking you in your apartment complex, and he lives there as well, then the law would say that he had a right to be there. Georgia law also states that, if he is in the course of doing his job, i.e., if he is a police officer on duty, or a journalist pursuing a story, he can't be prosecuted.

In order to gain a clear understanding of what conduct constitutes an offense under your state's statute, you can obtain a copy of it from your local law library. You also can find a listing of each state's stalking laws in the Internet section of the "Resources" at the back of this book. You may wish to consult with law enforcement officials, prosecutors, or a private attorney for an explanation and interpretation of the specific stalking statute in question.

In other words, stalking victims are often put in a position of having first to prove their case to a law enforcement official before being afforded the opportunity to prove their case before a court of law.

For this reason it is crucial for stalking victims to:

- Document every stalking incident as thoroughly as possible.
- Collect and keep any and all videotapes, audiotapes, answering machine messages, photos of the stalker, notes, letters, objects received from the stalker, eye witness affidavits, and records of property damage.
- Keep a journal to document all contacts and incidents, along with the time, date, and other relevant information such as location, anyone else present, any conversation that took place, etc.

Regardless of whether or not they have sufficient evidence to prove a stalking violation, victims wishing to file a stalking complaint with law enforcement officials should do so at the earliest possible point in time. In some cases, victims also may be able to file a complaint in the jurisdiction where the offender resides if it is different from the victim's.

If law enforcement officials refuse to investigate, or if they are not responsive to a complaint filed, victims may directly approach their local prosecutor (also known in various jurisdictions as the District Attorney, State's Attorney, Commonwealth's Attorney, or State Solicitor).

If you believe you are being stalked, seek assistance from the local domestic violence agency or rape crisis center. They can help you develop a personal safety plan in case you need it to escape.

The following information is a set of general actions you can take if you choose. Of course, your first step should always be to contact your local law enforcement agency.

If You Are in Imminent Danger

Your primary goal if you are in imminent danger should be to locate a safe place for yourself. Safety for stalking victims can often be found in the following places:

- Police stations
- Residences of family/friends that are unknown to the stalker
- Domestic violence shelters or local churches
- Public areas (stalkers may be less inclined toward violence or creating a disturbance in public places).

If departure from your current location is not possible, but a telephone is accessible, contact local law enforcement at 9-1-1 or any other law enforcement or emergency number. If the police do not indicate that they are sending an officer to you immediately, ask to speak to the police unit or division supervisor.

In dangerous situations, family members or friends can assist you in departing from your home or office. Always exercise caution, as stalking sometimes escalates into violence.

Upon reaching safety, you may want to communicate with law enforcement, victim services, mental health professionals and/or social services agencies in order to receive additional assistance and referrals available in your community. As a victim of stalking, you always should identify yourself as such and request confidentiality of all information given and any records kept or filed. If the stalker caused property damage or physical harm, you may choose to file a report with law enforcement immediately.

If You Are in Danger, But Not Immediately at Risk

If you determine that you are at risk for being in a potentially harmful or violent situation, the following options may be considered:

Restraining/Protective/Stay-Away Orders. Generally, these orders require the offender to stay away from—and not interfere with—the complainant. If violated, they may be punishable by incarceration, a fine, or both. These orders typically are obtained through a magistrate's office or local court. Contact the local Clerk of Court's office for information about where to obtain orders.

Reality Check: Restraining orders are not foolproof—they often do not extend beyond certain lines of jurisdiction, and can only be enforced if they are broken. Be careful not to develop a false sense of security.

In addition, some states only provide protective orders to former spouses or intimates. Moreover, it often costs money to obtain such an order due to the cost of filing fees, or in some courts and jurisdictions, due to the need of obtaining legal assistance. Orders are not assured—they are at the court's discretion.

Police Notification. If the perpetrator has broken the law by entering your residence without your permission, stealing and/or destroying your property, physically and/or sexually assaulting you, these acts may be punishable. Notifying police of illegal acts are important because: 1) if convicted, the perpetrator may be incarcerated and/or ordered to stay away from you; 2)charges may intimidate the offender, sending the message that his/her actions are illegal and will not be tolerated; and 3) filing a charge produces documentation, which may be useful in a future complaint for evidentiary or credibility purposes.

Documentation. Documentation of stalking should be saved and given to law enforcement. Documentation of the actions of the perpetrator may be useful in future complaints or proceedings, for evidentiary or credibility purposes. Documentation may take the form of photos of destroyed property/vandalism, photos of any injuries inflicted by the perpetrator, answering machine messages saved on tape, letters or notes written by the perpetrator, etc. You should keep a written log of any crimes or suspicious activities committed by the perpetrator. Use discretion when making entries, as the log may be used in court proceedings. Keep the log in a safe, secure location.

Contingency Plans. While you may not be in imminent danger, the potential always exists; therefore, a contingency plan may be appropriate. You may wish to keep a small packed suitcase in the trunk of your car or at another readily accessible location in case you decide against going home, or in case you need to depart your home suddenly.

Make sure you have access to critical telephone numbers, including:
• Law enforcement numbers and locations
• Safe places (such as friends, domestic violence shelters, etc.)
• Contact numbers for use after safety is secured (such as neighbors/family, attorneys, prosecutors, medical care, child care, pet care, etc.).

Reserve money may be necessary. Some stalkers have the means of ruining your credit and tying up your finances. You may need to have a financial reserve.

Keep other necessities with you, such as creditors' telephone numbers and personal welfare items such as medication, birth certificates, social security information, passports, etc.;

Miscellaneous Items. Always keep as full a tank of gas as possible in your car, and provide backup keys for neighbors. Inform people about your situation who may be useful in formulating a contingency plan, such as: law enforcement; employers; family, friends, or neighbors; and security personnel.

Nine Ways to Deal with Stalking

1. Install solid core doors with dead bolts in your home. If you cannot account for all keys, change the locks immediately and secure any and all spare keys.

2. Install adequate outside lighting. Trim back bushes and vegetation around your residence. Your lighting should shine out, away from the house. You can purchase motion-sensor lights that will come on when someone enters your property. Some of these lights also will signal interior lights to go on at the same time, alerting you that someone has penetrated your perimeter.

3. Maintain an unlisted phone number. If harassing calls persist, notify local law enforcement, but also keep a written log of harassing calls and

any answering machine tapes of calls with the stalker's voice and messages. If you have the financial means, use a "dummy" answering machine connected to a published phone line. The number to a private unlisted line can be reserved for close friends and family—the stalker never may realize that you have another telephone line.

4. Treat any threats as legitimate and inform law enforcement immediately.

5. Vary your travel routes, and the stores, restaurants, etc., that you use regularly. Limit time walking and jogging. You might have to walk/jog with a male friend or exercise indoors or at a club where access is limited.

6. Inform a trusted neighbor and/or colleagues about the situation. Provide them with a photo or description of the suspect and any vehicles he drives.

7. If residing in an apartment with an on-site property manager, provide the manager with a picture of the suspect. It is important to understand that if the stalker also lives in the apartment complex, you cannot, in most cases, file a stalking report against him in that area, since he has the right to be there.

8. Have co-workers screen all calls and visitors.

9. When out of the house or work environment, try not to travel alone if at all possible, and try to stay in public areas. If you ever need assistance, yell, "Fire," to get immediate attention, since people more readily respond to this cry for assistance than to any other.

Cyber-Stalking

The Internet and the World Wide Web have changed the way some women and men meet and develop relationships. Harassment can and does happen on the Internet and "cyber-stalking" is fast becoming a problem for women who are connected to the Web. The information in this section will give you some alternatives to protect your on-line privacy, and what options are open to you if you want to prosecute an online stalker.

Harassment on the Internet can be as threatening as any personal contact harassment. Just because you don't have a face-to-face stalking situation with the stalker, doesn't mean that you won't be unnerved, frightened, and in potential danger. Internet harassment is not just unsolicited email, but systematic and continually disturbing communication from an unwanted individual. These include:

- Unwanted/unsolicited email
- Unwanted/unsolicited talk requests
- Private or public messages posted on newsgroups
- Disturbing messages on usenet newsgroups or bulletin boards
- Unsolicited communications about you to co-workers, friends, and acquaintances
- Off-line communication such as paper mail or phone calls

Some law enforcement agencies don't take reports of online harassment and stalking as a serious threat, because they may believe that a woman can easily disconnect from the Internet if she is receiving disturbing communication. This can be true, but it may not be possible to totally disconnect from the Internet due to job requirements. It is also unreasonable to expect a woman to change her lifestyle so that the perpetrator can't get to her.

There are several ways to block unwanted communication, however it often is impossible to block all unsolicited emails and online harassment.

**Reality Check: Harassment on the Internet is
just as illegal as harassment in person.**

Cyber-Stalking Avoidance

Be cautious about with whom you communicate and what you reveal about yourself. The Internet is a great communication tool. It is also an anonymous tool. Not everything you read in an email is true. Many people lie about themselves during email conversations. Even if there's no immediate threat of physical danger on the Internet, you still have to be careful about the type of information you devulge. As with unsolicited telephone calls, you don't have to be nice to everyone and you don't have to get into a conversation with everyone who demands your attention. Make it a practice not to answer unsolicited email. If you feel at all uncomfortable with the conversation you're having with someone online, you have every right to stop all communication. Be even more careful whom you decide to meet in person. Friendships and professional relationships you start online can be beneficial relationships, but it's very difficult to predict what someone you have met online is like in person.

Reality Check: Dating from an Internet meeting can be very dangerous. Many people lie about themselves in chat rooms.

Check your personal information that might be on the Internet. This is stored in your user identification or attached to your name and address. Be careful of your personal information in filling out forms and credit applications. Be selective where you submit your name, address, phone number, picture, or work history. If you are looking for work, you increase your risk when you place your resume on the Internet. This is especially true if your address and phone number is attached to your job application and resume. You should be consistently curious about what information is online and remove those things that can lead a cyber-stalker to your front door. If you are online and use the Internet for email and other business and entertainment reasons, you need to be vigilant as to what kind of information you are making accessible to the public.

• Keep your user ID generic and guarded. Does your ID say that you are female?

• Change your signature file so that it does not contain personal information, such as your full name, address, workplace, or any of your phone numbers.

• Use the "Finger" Ultimate Directory (finger.com) on the Internet, to check into the amount of personal information that is available to the public. If you think Finger reveals too much about you, edit your file so that your privacy is protected.

• If you have a website, does it contain a photo, a resume, your name, address, work or home phone numbers, or does it list information about friends, family, or the area where you live? This information should be limited in scope.

• In your browser's HTML editor, you can check your Web page source code to make sure registration information (like your name) hasn't been inserted automatically by your HTML editor.

• Be cautious about posting information to Internet directories, bulletin boards, and other websites.

• Be your own private detective and investigate Internet search engines (Alta Vista, Yahoo, Excite, etc., usenet directories, and 4-1-1 phone directories) for your name.

• Could someone conceivably link your phone directory information to your online information and find out where you live?

• Once you have done your online homework, you then can program your browser to eliminate personal information being transferred during your connections to the Web. Consult your browser's user manual or help file, or call their technical support department for instructions on how to program your particular browser.

Actions to Take

If you are getting unsolicited email, ignore it. If the online stalker doesn't get a response from you, he may choose another victim.

Demand, in writing, that your stalker cease and desist. State that the communications are unwanted and inappropriate and that you will take further action if it does not stop. Don't worry about whether your letter sounds too harsh—make sure it's professional and to the point. Send the letter via registered mail. Make sure he has to sign for it and that you get back a written form that he received the letter. Put a copy of the letter you sent with the postal registration form in a safe place. If the stalking continues, have an attorney send a letter indicating that legal action will follow if the unwanted communication does not stop. After you send this mail, your communication with him must stop. Any further communication can feed his obsession. Remember that the harasser is looking for a sign from you that he is getting to you. Your attention to him is his reward and will fuel his attempts to harass you. It is common in a court case of harassment and stalking for the defendant to indicate the communication was not one-sided but consensual. If you file a harassment or stalking case, you will be expected to prove that the communication was definitely one-sided and unsolicited.

Document everything. Documentation should include every piece of email or other form of communication from this person, including all of the header information from an email or newsgroup posting. Also document how each communication is affecting your life, and what steps you are taking to remedy the situation.

If you are getting chat requests from an Internet Relay Chat (IRC) room like an AOL Instant Messenger, or any other type of communication, print it out, and write the date and time of the message. You might also indicate whether the message frightened you and how it affects you. Remember that the court will take into consideration how the communication affects the stalking victim. They will want to analyze whether the message is intimidating and how it is impacting your life. Before you file a complaint with the police, send copies of each harassing communication to your email's Webmaster and the harasser's email Webmaster. Each email server has a person who administers email traffic. Most email servers consider unsolicited emails and on-line harassment to be against their in-house ethical standards and will disconnect the harasser if he doesn't stop. This doesn't mean that he will stop, because he can easily get another email server and as long as he has your email address or website, he can start harassing you again. In addition to your archive of communications, start a log that explains the situation in more detail. Document how the harassment is affecting your life, and document what steps you're taking to stop it.

Report the situation to your friends, family, and co-workers. Tell friends or co-workers not to communicate with the harasser in any way. Inform your system administrator, your supervisor and work security personnel, as well as your apartment building's security people.

Report the situation to your local police. The FBI also will take a complaint, and will follow up on it if they have the manpower. Many states have modified their stalking laws to include electronic communications and will let you file a restraining order. You'll need the person's street address if you want to serve him with a restraining order or press charges against him. The police can get this information from the harasser's postmaster if they need to. The court may ask your harasser to reimburse you for any filing fees that you incurred if you win the case.

Change your password frequently. Pay attention to your files, directories, and last logout information. You may wish to stay out of any usenet or chat rooms that the stalker has frequented.

Remember that all harassment and stalking, whether via the Internet or face-to-face are potentially very dangerous. Assume the worst and take all necessary precautions as if your life depends on it.

chapter fifteen

dating and domestic violence

Dating and domestic violence, like rape, harassment, and stalking, are crimes of power and domination attributable to the same issues of male aggression. Violence inside an intimate relationship exists on a continuum of controlling behavior, ranging from verbal and emotional abuse to physical assault. In addition, this kind of violence is linked directly to the perpetrator having witnessed or experienced violence during his childhood. Batterers are everyday people of all races and socio-economic backgrounds.

Dating violence is a pattern of continual acts that threaten or physically or sexually abuse a partner while in a relationship.

Domestic violence is a pattern of continual acts that threaten or physically or sexually abuse a member of the abuser's household. This can be a spouse, ex-spouse, sibling, other relative, or resident of the home.

Dating violence and domestic violence both stem from the perpetrator's need for power and control and exist on a continuum of aggressive behaviors by the abuser. The dynamics of abuse and the victim's responses to the abuse are very similar in both dating and domestic violence situations.

In many cases, the only difference is that the victim of domestic violence is often economically dependent on the abuser. The victim may believe that she would be homeless and destitute without the financial support of the perpetrator. In dating violence situations, the victim is not generally dependent upon the abuser for shelter and financial support, however there may be a strong need for the financial or social benefits of being in an ongoing relationship with the abuser. Dating violence may begin as early as the teenage years. One in ten teenagers will experience some form of physical abuse in their dating relationships.

Many young people come to believe that love and abuse in relationships go hand and hand, especially because they may have little else with which to compare their experiences. They may downplay the physical abuse of their partner by making excuses for him. They may think that abusive or jealous behaviors are signs that their partners love them. This is especially true if being in a relationship is the most important thing in a young person's life. Young people in junior high school and high school can be obsessed with being popular. Popularity at this time of life often means having a date, going steady, or being in a relationship. When abuse starts to occur, friends may not encourage the victim to get help, because they believe this kind of behavior is normal or because they are also in abusive relationships and need to cover up the abuse. Unless they are exposed to healthy relationships, victims of dating violence often suffer needlessly, without the realization that the abuse is not acceptable, not normal, and certainly not their fault.

The movement to protect victims of domestic violence has many supporters and numerous laws, and improvements in law enforcement training have been made. However, for those young girls experiencing dating violence, there is not much support. The normal options for a victim of domestic violence—restraining orders, injunctions, arrest of the abuser—generally are not available in a dating violence situation because the victim may not be considered by law enforcement officials to be in imminent danger.

The Pattern of Teen Dating Violence

Dating violence generally exhibits a pattern of behavior with these common elements:

• Repeated violence will escalate into more abusive behavior.

• Violence will increase in severity the longer the relationship continues.

• Violence and abusive behaviors are followed with apologies and promises to change.

• Terminating the relationship increases the threats and level of violence for the victim.

Many times, the controlling behavior of the abuser will isolate the victim from her friends and make the possibility of getting help more difficult. She may feel increasingly alone and confused about how to escape the abuser. Teenagers in a dating violence situation may be reluctant to seek help from adults. They may distrust adults and be afraid of interference in the relationship. They also may be afraid that whatever independence they have will be taken away from them if they can't handle their own problems.

While drugs and alcohol do play a part in abuse, they are not a cause of the abuse. They may be an excuse, but are not a reason for the abuse.

Fifteen Warning Signs of Dating Violence

1. The man gets too serious about the relationship too quickly.
2. He is jealous and possessive, won't let you have friends, checks up on you, and won't accept breaking up.
3. He tries to control you by being very bossy, giving orders, and making all the decisions.
4. He humiliates you and belittles your opinions.
5. You are frightened of him and worry about how he will react to things you say or do.
6. He threatens you.

7. He is violent, has a history of fighting, loses his temper quickly, or brags about mistreating others. He may use or own weapons.

8. He pressures you for sex, or forces you to do sexual things that you don't want to do. He may attempt to manipulate you or lay a guilt-trip on you by saying, "If you really loved me you would..."

9. He expresses contempt for women, or treats them as sex objects.

10. He abuses drugs or alcohol and pressures you to take them with him even when you don't want to.

11. He blames you when he or others mistreat you and say that you provoked it.

12. He has a history of bad relationships and blames other people for his problems.

13. His statements or actions indicate that he thinks men should be in control and that women should do as they're told.

14. He has hit, pushed, choked, restrained, kicked, or physically hurt you.

15. Your family and friends have warned you about him or told you they were worried for your safety.

All too often, the abuser will blame the victim for the abuse. The guilt placed on the victim is a tremendous burden and is the primary cause for low self-esteem in victims. Perpetrators are always responsible for their actions. The abuse is not the fault of the victim.

People stay in abusive relationships for many reasons, however they don't stay because it really isn't that bad. Any abuse is bad abuse. There is no such thing as good abuse or justifiable abuse. Know the signs to watch for, and know how to prevent it. Again, prevention of this type of sexual assault will require a great deal of education.

Teen Dating Violence Prevention for Parents

Teach your teenager to protect herself. Help your teen—regardless of gender—become aware of the issues involved in teen dating violence. Encourage your teen to evaluate the safety of various situations. Brainstorm all possible ways of handling a situation, using events from the newspaper, experience of a friend, television, or movies. Help teens establish and develop self-awareness by encouraging them to think, choose, and make decisions for themselves.

Teach your teenager to be assertive. Assertiveness is the ability to exercise one's own rights while respecting the rights of others. It means communicating exactly what you want and don't want, standing up for yourself, and stating your opinions, thoughts, and feelings. Help your teen learn the difference between passive, assertive, and aggressive behavior. A self-defense course can develop assertiveness skills. Ask your teen, "Have you ever said, 'Yes,' when you wanted to say, 'No'?" Practice what the teen could say or do if given another chance.

Help your teenager understand what a healthy relationship is. Point out features of healthy relationships from books, movies, or real life. In addition to feelings of love, emphasize the following characteristics of healthy relationships:

• Both partners give and take, each getting their way some of the time and compromising some of the time.

• Partners respect each other, and value each other's opinion.

• They support and encourage each other in their individual goals and ambitions.

• They trust one another. Jealousy is not healthy and is not part of a healthy relationship.

• Neither one is afraid of the other person.

• They communicate openly and honestly, and make their partners feel safe in expressing their opinion, even when it differs with the other partner.

• They share responsibility in decision-making.

• They accept the differences between them, and don't try to control the relationship.

• They encourage each other to have friends and activities outside the relationship.

• Each partner tries their best to be supportive, caring, and respectful of the other person's wishes.

Domestic Violence

The difference between domestic violence and violence that takes place in a dating relationship is slight. However, an adult victim of domestic violence may have had several dating relationships that were violent prior to her present violent relationship. This factor may have caused her to have less self-esteem and it also may have conditioned her to believe that all normal relationships are violent and abusive. She may feel less hopeful, more isolated, and more adept at covering up the abuse and making excuses for her abusive partner.

Reality Check: In 1992, 7 percent of American women (3.9 million) who were married or living with someone as a couple were physically abused; 37 percent (20.7 million) were verbally or emotionally abused by their partner or spouse.

Each year, millions of women are abused by their partners. Very few victims will tell anyone, including friends, relatives, neighbors, or the police. Victims of domestic violence come from all cultures, income groups, ages, and religions. They share common feelings of helplessness, isolation, guilt, fear, and shame. When a woman feels trapped in a violent relationship, often the greatest hurdle that she can overcome is denial. At some point, she first will have to accept the situation as it is, without sugarcoating it or pretending that it isn't a problem. She also will have to come to the reality that her partner's promises to change and never abuse her again are false.

She may not have anyone who can help her come to this conclusion, and if she hasn't sought support, it will be her own decision. Many times, battered women will put up with the abuse as long as their children are not threatened. Once the children are in danger, the mother's, protective nature towards their children gives her enormous courage and they will finally leave.

Steps to Freedom

Don't ignore the problem, or make excuses to yourself about his behavior.

Talk to someone. Part of the abuser's power comes from secrecy. Victims often are ashamed to let anyone know about intimate family problems.

Go to a friend or neighbor, or call a domestic violence hotline.

Plan ahead and know what you will do if you are attacked again.

If you decide to leave, choose a safe place to go.

Set aside some money.

Put important papers—marriage license, birth certificates, and checkbooks—in a place where you can get them quickly.

Learn to think independently.

Try to plan for the future and set goals for yourself.

All of the above steps should be done discreetly, without the abuser's knowledge. Do not let him know you are thinking about leaving or getting help.

Be careful not to leave domestic violence literature around the house where he may find it. If he finds out what your plans are, he may close your bank account, restrict your access outside the house, or even hold your children hostage so that you don't leave him.

If You Are Hurt, What Can You Do?

There are no easy answers, but there are things you can do to protect yourself. As with a stalker, a person who commits continual domestic violence gets more dangerous as the possibility of losing his "property" looms closer and closer. You should realize that this kind of criminal might not honor any restraining order or verbal warning from the police or a judge. You may have to get a weapon and learn to use it to protect yourself. I rarely recommend lethal weapons for most potential victims, but in this case, it may come down to either you physically stopping him or him killing you and your family. Make sure to follow all of these steps first:

• Call the police or sheriff. Assault, even by family members, is a crime. The police often have information about shelters and other agencies that help victims of domestic violence.

• Leave, or have someone come and stay with you.

• Go to a battered women's shelter—call a crisis hotline in your community or a health center to locate a shelter. If you believe that you, or your children, are in danger, leave immediately.

• Get medical attention from your doctor or a hospital emergency room. Ask the staff to photograph your injuries and keep detailed records in case you decide to take legal action.

• Contact your family court for information about a civil protection order that does not involve criminal charges or penalties.

Reality Check: There are no guarantees. There are risks to leaving as well as staying.

Many people don't understand why women stay with abusive men. There are many factors as to why people stay in abusive relationships; from economic dependency, children, lack of realistic options, and lack of self-esteem. Whatever the reason for staying, there can only be one reason to leave—you do not deserve to be abused and mistreated.

If you stay, the abuse almost certainly will get worse. The violence will escalate. If you leave, you also may enrage the abuser and he may become more violent if he can get to you. This is why you definitely will need all the professional help you can get—therapists, domestic violence shelters, counselors, law enforcement authorities—to help you escape. I urge you to take action and contact the appropriate domestic violence contact numbers in the "Resources" section of this book. You are not alone. There are many other women who have been in your situation who can assist you in making the right decision for you and your family.

section four

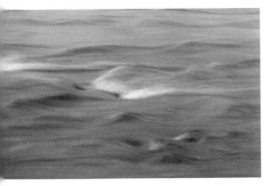

what men must know

chapter sixteen

advice for men

It is time for men to change, time for us to halt rape, sexual harassment, stalking, and domestic violence. Men can no longer keep silent while others continue their rampage. Men absolutely have to change the way they live and interact with others. If you're a man or boy reading this chapter, you must consider that if you do nothing to stop the violence, then you are part of the problem. Take a look at these statistics and consider your responsibility to do something to change yourself and other men:

- One in five college women survive rape or attempted rape.
- 84 percent of survivors know their attacker.
- 57 percent of rapes happen on dates.
- 92 percent of the time, a woman reporting a rape is telling the truth.
- 75 percent of men and 55 percent of women involved in acquaintance rape are drinking or taking drugs just before the attack.
- One in twelve men admit to committing acts that meet the legal definition of rape or attempted rape.
- 42 percent of rape survivors tell no one about the rape.
- 84 percent of rape survivors try unsuccessfully to reason with the rapist.

Although this book is primarily for women, I could not write a book about date rape without saying something to men as well. We live in a highly sexualized society and women have not yet achieved full equality. It seems to me almost impossible to grow up as a male in this society and not to think about or fantasize about the act of rape. Does that someone who does think such thoughts a rapist? No. We all have thoughts and fantasies of a sexual nature that we wouldn't want made public.

In the course of my work to eliminate rape in our society, I have presented crime prevention seminars to hundreds of thousands of people. I ran into a series of common responses from a man's perspective. Men's questions and responses centered on two main issues:

1. Their concerns about women who lead them on, flirt heavily with them, and then, when the man has reached his sexual peak, say no to sexual intercourse.

2. Their concern that women may be claiming to have been raped in order to get even with a man or to hurt him and ruin his reputation.

The first statement implies that a man is not really responsible for his actions beyond a certain point and that if a woman wants to avoid getting raped, she shouldn't turn a man on to such a degree that he can't stop himself. In questioning men about their ability to control their sexual arousal, I asked them if there had been any occasion in their lives when they suddenly had to stop during intercourse? In one case, a young man had been fondling his girlfriend when her mother came home unexpectedly, surprising him in the act. What was interesting about this situation is that the girl had tried to get him to stop repeatedly without success. He said, *"I'm too turned on to stop now,"* but when her mother walked in on them, he somehow found the self-control to stop immediately. In fact, he said his erection was gone almost at once.

Reality Check: There is no point at which a man cannot control himself during sexual arousal. He may not want to control himself, but he can stop.

Let's make this a bit more personal and take it a step further. Suppose you (a man) were out of work, had no money, hadn't worked for a long time, and money was all you could think about. You dreamed about it every night. Your creditors were banging on your door and harassing you on a daily basis. You had to have some money. So you went to a bank and asked for a loan, which the bank refused. You then went up to the teller's window and watched her count the money on the other side of the counter. When you felt as if you couldn't take it anymore, you grabbed a handful of bills from the teller and ran out of the bank.

Did you commit a crime? Would the bank prosecute you? Would you expect to go to jail if caught? I hope you would answer yes, because you did indeed break the law and the consequences for your actions are that you will go to a state prison for a number of years. Do you see the analogy? If we use the example of robbing a bank, then perhaps you can see that even though you needed the money and were in debt, you still committed a crime! Even though you felt the bank "tempted you" with all that money lying around, you still took what did not belong to you and committed a felony. Can you logically say that the bank caused you to commit robbery, because it was enticing you with its financial reserves? The tellers even had the audacity to count the money in the open. Likewise, you could say that if they didn't want to get robbed, then they shouldn't have been so provocative with their money.

In the same manner, when you are physically turned on, that does not give you the right to take what doesn't belong to you. You may feel that your date shouldn't be a tease and turn you on, or that she should not drink and get you worked up so that you do not want to stop. If you don't like the way you are being treated, and if you feel like she is manipulating you, then get up and leave. You are in control. You always have a choice. It doesn't matter what you think at this point. We all have had fantasies of robbing a bank and getting away with it. No one will put you in jail for robbing a bank in your mind, but the minute you decide to act out your fantasy, you have committed a crime and can go to jail. It's the same in a rape situation. The minute you take action and force sex with someone against her will, or without her conscious consent, you have committed the crime of rape and can go to jail.

Reality Check: If you are obsessed with thoughts of rape, you should seek professional help from a psychologist, psychiatrist, or school counselor, to stop the momentum of your thoughts from turning into actions.

Beyond getting caught and what happens to you, think about the woman. The minute you physically commit rape, you have abused a woman and possibly scarred her for the rest of her life.

Following are some of the common misperceptions, misunderstandings, and myths that many men harbor:

Myth: If she didn't struggle, it wasn't rape.

Fact: Rape is sex without consent, whether there is a struggle or not.

Myth: If she goes along with it, it isn't rape.

Fact: Rape is rape if she feels she has no choice or is incoherent or unconscious.

Myth: If she didn't scream, it wasn't rape.

Fact: The greatest fear in a rape victim is the fear of being killed. She may not scream because she is too frightened.

Myth: If she had sex before, or has sex frequently, it wasn't rape or she deserved it.

Fact: Her sexual history and yours with or without her has nothing to do with this situation. Prior consent is not necessarily current consent.

Myth: Women are to blame for rape if they are in "risky situations."

Fact: A woman is no more to blame for being raped because she was in a risky situation, than a deer is for wandering into the sights of the hunter. Remember, the criminal is at fault, not the victim!

Myth: Women who wear attractive clothes should expect to be raped.

Fact: What she wears has nothing to do with the behavior of the rapist.

Rape is about power, not sex. Babies and senior citizens also get raped. Do we question the suggestiveness of baby attire or an old person's clothing? Of course not. This is just another method of shifting the blame from the criminal to the victim.

Criminals start a life of crime in their thoughts before their actions get them into trouble with the law. You are or will become what you consistently think about. As men, we must all take responsibility for our own thoughts and actions.

Reality Check: No one turns you on. You turn yourself on with the thoughts that are going on inside your head.

The thoughts are yours, not hers. You have control over them, she doesn't. You can change your thoughts. You can continue to think about her, about how you want to "make it with her," and get yourself all worked up so that your conscience cannot reach you anymore. Realize that only you turn yourself on, and only you turn yourself off.

It's time to stop blaming women and others for men's actions. Men are in control. Men do the deed. Men break the law. It is men who have the problem with violence. You may be thinking, "What about women? Don't women rape? Don't women stalk? Don't women sexually harass? Don't women commit domestic violence?" Yes. But the statistics indicate that the vast majority of crimes of violence are committed by men, not women. So, it's men. Men have the problem, and it's up to us to stop it.

After She Says No, It's Rape!

If you have sex with someone who cannot give consent due to being incapacitated by alcohol or drugs or is otherwise unconscious, you have committed rape!

If you have sex with someone and get her unwilling consent or lack of resistance due to your verbal, physical, or emotional threats, then you have made it impossible for her to say, "No," therefore you have committed rape. Can she change her mind? Yes. If she originally wanted to have sex, and at the last minute decides she no longer wants to go through with it, it is her right to say, "No," and to stop it, just as it is your right. A man has the same right to "pull out" in the middle of intercourse, regardless of whether a woman wants to continue or not. So a woman has the same right to stop, regardless of your desires and wants at the moment.

You break the law when you persist in your sexual advances after she has said, "No." It is also rape if she is incapacitated so that her ability to say, "no," is impaired.

Many men fear the possibility that a woman may be manipulating them into a sexual situation only to change her mind on a whim. Is this a real problem? Sometimes, women do manipulate men to get what they want from them. Of course, men do the same thing. If you feel that a woman is teasing you and playing with your emotions, rather than risk a potential rape situation with her, sit down and talk to her. Tell her exactly what you feel and that you're confused by her inconsistent behavior.

You might say:

"Look, I don't appreciate the way I'm being treated."

"I'm getting a lot of mixed messages from you. It seems one minute you want to have sex and the next minute you don't. What's going on?"

"I want you to know that this is your decision too and I'm not going to take advantage of you. Please be honest with me and tell me what you want. Yes or no."

Many men also are concerned that a woman would attempt to ruin a man's reputation by making up a rape story.

Reality Check: No person in her right mind would fabricate a rape charge and go through all of the terror and trauma of reporting it to the police, taking the evidentiary exam and exposing herself to the aftermath of insinuations and abuse by friends, family, and the judicial system, unless something had occurred.

Many men also are concerned that a woman would attempt to ruin a man's reputation by making up a rape story.

It's hard for some men to grasp what a woman goes through at the time of the rape with the ongoing trauma that can last for years, unless he has himself been raped or been touched by the rape of a sister or close friend.

For some men, thinking about rape can be a pleasant sexual fantasy. To them, rape is being ravished by several women and satiated until they're exhausted. The pain that in reality goes along with an actual rape is generally missing from the male fantasy. Women rarely rape men. Some do, but the real threat for men is not being raped by women, but by other men. If you remember that rape is an act of aggression and power, not sex, then maybe you can see yourself as a potential victim.

Imagine yourself going out with a bunch of guys. Maybe you all go to a football game. You have a great time and afterwards you all go to a local bar for more than a few drinks. On the way home, something happens and these guys who you thought were your friends, suddenly turn on you and attack. They take you to a vacant lot, beat you up, and decide to rape you. You fight like hell, but you're outnumbered. They hold you down and brutally rape you for four or five hours. They punch you and kick you, all the while telling you how much you're enjoying it. Then it's over. They tell you that if you ever tell anyone, they'll come back and kill you. After they leave you lying on the ground, hurt and bleeding, you finally get up and make your way to a gas station where you try to tell the attendants about what happened. They laugh and call you a drunk and other epithets. Then they tell you to get lost. You finally get to a police station. They are skeptical and ask whether you're a homosexual. You can hear them snickering behind your back. They say, "There's no way I'd let any guy do that to me. I'd kill him first." Another one says, "I'd kill myself first." They keep asking you why you didn't fight back? You try to explain that there were four of them and that there was no way to stop them. They take the report, but you sense that they won't be doing anything about it.

Telling your girlfriend is a big mistake. She thinks you must have done something to provoke the incident. Then she starts wondering about your sexuality, or whether you've cheated on her. You can feel her getting colder to you, and you think that maybe she thinks that this was all your fault.

Now you know you can never tell your parents. Your mom might understand, but there's no way your father could ever handle it.

Your pain does not end there. You have difficulty sleeping nights and the guys who raped you call you from time to time to threaten you if you decide to tell anyone. The fear and anxiety are keeping you a prisoner in your own apartment. You decide to drop the case and tell the police you don't want to prosecute. You know that because you all had several drinks together, everyone would think you invited the attack. You feel like you are all alone.

No one understands the pain and humiliation that you are going through and for the first time in your life, you contemplate suicide. If only someone would believe you!

Then one day a woman comes up to you and tells you she is from the women's support group on campus. She says she would like to talk to you. You're reluctant, but she confides that like you, she too was a victim of rape. She puts you in touch with the rape crisis center counselor. After a while, you join a support group of other rape victims, some of them are men, and for the first time since the assault, you know you are not alone, that you are not the only victim of rape. Now the long healing process begins.

Does this sound impossible? Although it was a gang rape, the aftermath, where the victim can't get support from those to whom she turns for help, is actually a very common date/acquaintance rape scenario.

Rape, date/acquaintance rape, sexual assault, stalking, sexual harassment, and domestic violence are all crimes of power. The primary reason for the abuse is to gain power. This power is taken from another person through deception, intimidation, and physical force.

Reality Check: Remember that rape is a crime of power not sex, so whether you're a male or female, it can happen to you.

In reality, most abusers have very low self-esteem. Their lives are out of control and they feel powerless to change things, so instead of looking within to find an inner sense of personal power, which is the only kind that lasts, they look outside themselves, mistakenly feeling that the only way to get power is from another person. This belief is not valid, and will not make you feel more powerful.

So why don't rapists try to steal power from other men? Because rapists are generally cowardly individuals who feel inferior to other men. They can only steal power from someone "lesser" than they are. They will attack a woman, young girl, or older female, i.e., one who appears vulnerable, weak, and alone. That's why women who have great personal power and confidence are not as likely to be attacked. These women present themselves as more formidable adversaries. In the field of crime prevention, we would say they are hardened targets, instead of soft targets.

Preventing rape is, in reality, the responsibility of all men. But rape is not just an act of violence that occurs out of nowhere, it has its causes and sources. As in all physical behavior, rape starts in the mind. In order to change the behavior, we must change the thoughts that created it.

Over the centuries, women have become objects; objects to be wanted, desired, taken, and used. Anything that objectifies women creates and maintains a society that supports rape ideas.

Some Advice for Men

Know your sexual desires and limits. Communicate them clearly.
Be aware of social pressures.
It's OK not to "score."
Being turned down when you ask for sex is not in any way a rejection of you personally.

Women who say "No" to sex are not rejecting you; they are expressing their desire not to participate in a single act.

Your desires may be beyond your control, but your actions are well within your control.

Accept the woman's decision. "No" means "No."

Don't read other meanings into the answer...even based on past experience with this or other women.

Don't continue after "No." If you're thinking the woman doesn't mean it, simply stop and ask...then respect her decision.

Don't assume that just because a woman dresses in a sexy manner and flirts that she wants to have sexual intercourse.

Don't assume that previous permission for sexual contact applies to the current situation.

Avoid excessive use of alcohol and/or drugs.

There is an epidemic of violence in relationships, and it's all about control. Relationships run by control and/or violence are unhealthy and harmful to both individuals, and will never be as rewarding as a healthy, loving relationship.

Men can change their attitudes and behavior and can see that treating women respectfully and equitably has great benefits for men as well. I have been in many conversations with men who have begun to see that they may have forced themselves on a non-consenting woman at one time or another. The man still may be involved with or know the woman. If it occurs to you as you are reading this book that you have hurt someone in this way, you can get help and break the cycle. I encourage you to do so, as your life will be transformed for the better in the process. Here is how to begin:

- Realize that your behavior is covering up insecurity and that you damage your family, your relationships, and yourself when you act in a violent manner.

- Be aware that you break the law when you physically hurt someone.
- Take responsibility for your actions and get help.
- When you feel tension building, get away.
- Work off angry energy through a walk, a project, or a sport.
- Call a domestic violence hotline or health center and ask about counseling and support groups.

Breaking Up

A time of great vulnerability is when a relationship is coming to an end. Most dating and domestic violence occur when the relationship is breaking up. The breaking up experience can be very difficult for both parties. Below is a list of "Do's" and "Don'ts" that may help make breaking up easier to go through.

Do

Explain your reasons for breaking up if you can

Be respectful and listen

Find ways to take care of your feelings: Keep a journal, talk to friends, exercise, play sports, listen to music, allow yourself to cry

Seek counseling

Don't

Threaten

Have sex one last time

Follow the other person to see if he or she is going out with someone

Call unless you've both agreed this is OK

Break up to scare the person into doing things your way

Get even

Try to get pregnant or cause a pregnancy

Call names, spread rumors, or otherwise try to get revenge

Isolate yourself, be alone

Assume being friends means you will get back together

Love

There are certain images and words describing what love is that lead to confusion and sometimes to bad situations. In fact, some of these messages are actually what love isn't. There are many things about love that can't be summed up in a word. Here are two lists to help you sort out what love is or isn't. These lists are to help you decide how you want to be treated.

LOVE IS . . .	LOVE ISN'T . . .
Responsibility	Jealousy
Hard Work	Possessiveness
Pleasure	Pain
Commitment	Violence
Caring	Obsession
Honesty	Being selfish
Trust	Cruelty
Communication	Getting pregnant
Sharing	Making someone pregnant
Compromising	Dependency
Closeness	Giving up who you are
Recognizing differences	Intimidation
Vulnerability	Scoring
Openness	Fear
Respect	Proving yourself
Friendship	Manipulation
Strong positive feelings	Expecting all your needs to be met

Conflict

Some men find it extremely difficult to deal with conflict. Conflict is part of everyday life. You can't always avoid conflict but you can learn to manage it without violence. Following are some of the skills you need to manage personal conflict.

Understand your own feelings about conflict. This means recognizing your "triggers," words or actions that immediately provoke an emotional response, like anger. It could be a facial expression, a tone of voice, a pointing finger, a certain phrase. Once you know your "triggers," you can better control your emotions.

Practice active listening. Go beyond hearing just words—try to understand what the other person is really saying. Listen carefully, instead of thinking about what you're going to say next. Active listening requires concentration and body language that says you are paying attention and care about what the other person has to say.

Generate options for resolving a conflict. Many people can think of only two ways to manage conflict—fighting or avoiding the problem. Get the facts straight, brainstorm all ideas that might help resolve the argument, and discuss the pros, cons, and consequences of continuing such a disagreement. If you're left with raging emotions that lead to more problems, then your style isn't working. Try to learn new conflict resolution techniques. There are many personal growth programs that can give you a toolbox for communicating better and avoiding confrontation. Call your local community college, or talk to friends or religious leaders who can help of refer to someone who can.

State your needs and define the problem. Talk about the issues without insulting or blaming the other person. Don't state your position; that's simply your solution to the problem. Before you can resolve a problem, you have to agree about what the problem is. Get to the root of the conflict before you start looking for a solution. Take a look at what is said and what is really needed.

Together, discuss various ways of meeting needs or solving the problem. Be flexible and open-minded. Decide who will be responsible for a specific action after reaching agreement on a plan.

Tips for Making Peace

Choose a convenient time to have a discussion.
Plan ahead.
Talk directly.
Don't blame or name-call.
Give information.
Listen.
Show that you are listening.
Talk through the issues.
Work on a solution.
Follow through.
If you can't work it out, get help.

There is no excuse for not getting help. There are hundreds of rape and violence prevention centers around the country and in Canada that are geared to helping men prevent violence against women. There is a partial list of centers in the "Resources" section of this book that can help you whether you are a batterer, a survivor of battering, or whether you have a problem with forced sexual contact. Getting help does not make you less of a man. It means you have the courage to know when an objective viewpoint is needed.

I urge you to have the courage to be part of the solution by standing up for non-violence, and not to be part of the problem by remaining silent.

resources

National and Local Crisis Hotlines

In a situation of danger or imminent danger, always call 9-1-1 or another emergency number. To begin to assemble the resources to cope after an assault has taken place, below are national crisis hotlines. You can find similar hotlines in your local Yellow Pages, usually listed under "Crisis Intervention." Most larger cities and colleges have rape crisis centers. Many of these crisis intervention lines specialize in helping men stop committing rape and violence. Most women have support groups and friends and are knowledgeable about how to find their local rape crisis center. Please contact your local telephone directory or information for the rape crisis center and other intervention telephone numbers.

National Crisis Hotlines:

Abuse and Assault 800-962-2873

Citizen Complaint Center, Civil Rights Division 202-514-4718

Crime Victims' Counseling Services 718-875-5862

AIDS All Prevention 800-322-8911

AIDS HIV 800-342-2437

Ask a Nurse (24 hr. free medical advice) 800-535-1111

"How to end domestic violence in your community" kit 800-777-1960

National Coalition Against Sexual Assault 717-232-7460

National Domestic Violence Hotline 800-799-7233

National Resource Center on Domestic Violence 800-537-2238

Family Violence Prevention Fund 415-252-8900

National Organization for Victim Assistance 202-232-6682

National Victim Center 703-276-2880

R.A.I.N.N. (Rape Abuse Incest National Network)
 800-656-HOPE (ext. 1)

Victim Services Hotline 213-485-6976

State by State Hotlines and Resources

ALASKA

Anchorage
Men's Center Inc. 907-272-4822

Male Awareness Program
907-272-0100

Juneau
Alternatives to Violence
907-586-3585

Council on Domestic Violence
907-465-4356

CALIFORNIA

Bell
Aztian Family Clinic 213-560-9992

Berkeley
Center for Non-Abusive Relationships
510-452-6243

Canoga Park
Counseling West 818-999-6164

Nueva Esperanza 818-898-0223

Valley Center for Prevention of
Family Violence 800-290-2079

Carlsbad
Homepeace 619-969-0515

Cerritos
American Family Alliance
800-348-9297

Chula Vista
Chula Vista Intervention Team
619-420-3620

YWCA Domestic Violence Treatment
Program 619-270-4504

City of Industry
Twin Palms Recovery Center
818-968-8875

Concord
Domestic Violence Treatment
Program 510-930-8300

Covina
Cirtus Counseling Domestic Violence
Program 818-967-7585

Santa Anita Family Services
818-966-1755

Davis
Alternatives to Violence Crisis Line
916-758-8400

Diamond Bar
Generation Foundation
909-594-9432

El Cajon
Professional Community Services
619-449-8703

El Monte
Acacia Counseling 818-335-6114

Casa Blanca Community Services
818-444-6204

Latino Domestic Violence Program
818-444-6204

Pathways Family Domestic Violence
Services 818-350-4029

Project Info. Community Services
818-442-4788

Twin Palms Recovery Center
818-443-4008

Encinitas
Association for Domestic Violence
619-565-8303

Escondido
EYE: Counseling & Crisis Services
619-747-6281

La Mesa Counseling Domestic
Violence
619-740-0287

Palomar Domestic Violence Response
Program 619-745-3811

Eureka
Alternatives to Violence
707-443-7358

Felton
Alternatives to Violence
408-335-3110

Ft. Bragg
People's Alternatives to Violence
707-964-7461

Fresno
Marjorie Mason Center
209-233-4357

Gardena
Behavorial Health Services
310-679-9031

The Counseling Center
310-324-0444

Glendale
Diversion—The First Step
818-988-2597

Counseling Center 818-547-2865

Family Services 818-248-2286

Humanistic Psychological Center
818-242-6424

New Horizons Psychological Center
818-545-9848

New Insights Program
818-242-2308

Time Out: A Batterer's Treatment
Program 818-409-9723

Glendora
Acacia Counseling 818-335-6114

Community Education Center
818-335-0411

Inglewood
Anderson & Anderson 310-208-5069

Batterer's Treatment Program
310-674-6215

Family Services of Long Beach
310-436-9893

La Mesa
Domestic Violence Program
619-697-7654

La Mesa Counseling Domestic
Violence Program
619-463-9742

Lancaster
Cedarwood Counseling Group
805-945-7608

High Road Program 805-942-2241

Lawndale
Anderson & Anderson 310-208-5069

Lomita
HPI Counseling Center
310-530-5654

Long Beach
Alternatives to Violence
310-493-1161

American Family Alliance
800-348-9297

Counseling Center 310-324-0444

Fred Kennedy Associates
310-986-5046

La Clinica Para Su Ayuda
800-782-9832

Options Counseling 310-989-0809

Saddle Group Counseling
310-427-2323

Los Angeles
About Face: Domestic Violence
Intervention Project 213-384-7084

Abuse Prevent Program
213-937-1344

Anderson & Anderson 310-208-5069

Another Way 310-645-2665

Behavioral Health Services
213-221-1746

California Diversion Intervention
Foundation 800-842-9089

Catholic Psychological Services
213-251-3569

Central Recovery Project
213-732-2098

CGI-Counseling Center
310-209-0904

Center Against Abusive Behavior
213-734-3494

Coalition of Mental Health
213-777-3120

El Centro Human Services Center
213-265-9228

Family Services Agency
818-845-7671

Family Services of LA Metro
213-381-3626

King Drew Domestic Violence
Batterer's Treatment 213-564-6982

Psychological Services 310-208-5069

Southern California Counseling
Center 213-937-1344

Sunrise Community Counseling
Center 213-368-3550

Victory Foundation 818-842-9446

Women's Center 310-246-0354

Wrap Agency 310-337-1550

Mission Hills
CPS Domestic Violence Program
800-770-7387

Monrovia
Santa Anita Family Services
818-359-9358

Monterey
Men's Alternatives to Violence
408-443-6288

Napa
Man Alive Alternatives to Violence
707-258-1778

Newhall
Association to Aid Victims of
Domestic Violence 805-259-8175

CPS Domestic Violence Program
800-770-7387

North Highlands
Changing Courses 916-332-5056

North Hills
Stephen Fleisher 818-993-9311

Northridge
Domestic Abuse Center
818-772-0176

Norwalk
California Intervention Foundation
800-842-9089

Oakland
Center for Non-Abusive Relationships
510-452-6243

Oceanside
Domestic Violence Treatment
Program
619-757-3500

Pacoima
Diversion—The First Step
818-988-2597

Valley Prevention & Treatment Center
818-896-1433

Palos Verdes Peninsula
Project Cool 310-544-0016

Pasadena
Center Against Abusive Behavior
818-796-7358

Foothill Family Services
818-795-6907

High Road Program 818-793-6159

I Am Foundation 310-907-9013

Pomona
Community Crisis Center
909-623-1588

Inland Valley Recovery Services—
Domestic Violence 909-865-2255

Rialto
Molesters/Batterers Anonymous
909-355-1100

Sacramento
Asian Resources Inc. 916-424-8960

California Child, Youth & Family
Coalition 916-739-6912

Diogenes Youth Services
916-363-0064

Interfaith Service Bureau, Violence
Prevent Task Force 916-456-3815

WEAVE Alternatives to Violencecrisis
line 916-920-2952

Salinas
Men's Alternatives to Violence
408-443-6288

San Diego
Corrigan Family Safety Project
619-565-8303

Family Services Center, Marine Corps
619-524-5728

Domestic Violence Prosecution Unit
619-533-5644

Episcopal Domestic Violence
Treatment 619-688-2440

EYE: Counseling & Crisis Services
619-747-6281

Family Life Domestic Violence
Treatment Services 619-529-9616

Family Services Center
619-524-5728

Family Violence Recovery Program
619-544-1453

First Unitarian Church Stopping
Gender Violence Project
619-298-9978

Fox Domestic Violence Treatment
Program 619-293-3007

Institute Domestic Violence Treatment
Program 619-688-1035

Standards for Treatment of Offenders
619-533-3000

YWCA Domestic Violence Treatment
619-270-4504

San Fernando
North Valley Counseling Center
818-365-8588

Nueva Esperanza 818-347-8565

Manalive Alternatives to Violence
415-239-8050

Men Overcoming Violence
415-777-4496

San Francisco
Pocovi on Valencia 415-552-1361

San Jose
Family Services Domestic Violence
Project 408-288-6200

San Pedro
Fred Kennedy Associates
310-833-3521

San Rafael
Alternatives to Violence
415-924-1070

Santa Cruz
Men's Alternatives to Violence
408-425-5248

Santa Fe Springs
Lacada 310-906-2676

Southeast Area Counseling Center
310-868-9919

Santa Monica
TEAM 310-556-2050

Santa Rosa
Alternatives to Violence
707-528-2636

Santee
Domestic Violence Treatment
Program 619-449-9937

COLORADO

Adams City
AMEND 303-429-7144

Aurora
AMEND 303-220-1911

Boulder
AMEND 303-444-8064

Colorado Springs
AMEND 719-633-1462

Denver
AMEND 303-832-6365

Lakewood
AMEND 303-987-3444

Long Mont
AMEND 303-441-8060

CONNECTICUTT

Bridgeport
Inner City Violence Prevention Project
203-384-0011

Men & Stress,
YMCA 203-334-5551

DISTRICT OF COLUMBIA

Washington
Men's Rape Prevention Project
202-265-6530

Men's Anti-Rape Residence Center
301-386-2737

National Coalition Against Domestic
Violence 202-638-6388

National Council on Child Abuse &
Family Violence 800-222-2000

GEORGIA

Athens

Ending Violence & Abuse Toward Women 706-369-0078

Rape Crisis Center Metro Area 706-353-1912

Atlanta

Crisis Intervention 404-659-8505

Crisis Management International Counseling Centers 404-841-3400

Crisis Resource Center 404-221-0252

Kidspeace National Centers For Kids In Crisis 770-719-0808

Men Living Without Violence 404-933-7789

Men Stopping Violence 404-688-1376

Rape Crisis Center/Grady Memorial Hospital 404-616-4861

Augusta

Richmond County Rape Crisis Line 706-821-1261

Rape Crisis Services 706-724-5200

Crisis Line 706-560-2943

Clayton

Rape Crisis Center 770-477-2177

Columbus

Cornerstone Crisis Stabilization Program 706-323-7095

Crisis Center 706-327-3999

Kidspeace National Center 706-561-498

Dekalb

Rape Crisis Center 404-377-1428

Georgia State Community Support Services 706-369-6188

Fulton County

Emergency Mental Health Services 404-730-1600

Jonesboro

Rape Crisis Center 770-477-2177

Macon

Crisis Group Home 912-322-4000

Marietta

Rape Crisis Center Cobb County YWCA 770-428-2666

Savannah

Rape Crisis Center 912-233-7273

ILLINOIS

Chicago

Men's Anger Network 312-643-5477

INDIANA

Ft. Wayne

Center for Nonviolence 219-4456-4112

KANSAS

Arkansas City

Cowley County Mental Health 316-442-4540

MASSACHUSETTS

Amherst

Men's Resource Center 413-253-9887

Arlington

Ending Men's Violence 617-648-5957

Ashfield
Men's Alternatives to Violence
413-628-4770

Brookline
Real Men 617-782-7838

Cambridge
EMERGE 617-422-1548

Haydenville
Stop It Now 413-268-3096

Sudbury
Victim Advocacy Network
508-820-0390

MARYLAND

Baltimore
Anti-Sexist Collective 410-243-1109

Sexual Assault/Domestic Violence
Center 410-377-8111

MICHIGAN

Traverse City
Time Out Program 616-947-6800

Ypsilanti
Alternatives to Domestic Aggression
313-484-1260

MINNESOTA

Duluth
Domestic Abuse Intervention
218-722-2781

Minneapolis
Brother Peace 612-929-5713

Domestic Abuse Project
612-874-7063

Sexual Violence Center
612-871-5111

MISSOURI

Columbia
Bravo 314-875-1370

Kansas City
Alternatives to Anger 816-753-5118

St. Louis
RAVEN 314-647-4357

St. Charles County
Developing Options to Violence
314-946-2815

NEW HAMPSHIRE

Concord
New Hampshire Coalition Against
Domestic & Sexual Violence
603-224-8893

NEW MEXICO

Las Cruces
Quaker Witness Program
505-521-4260

NEW YORK

Buffalo
Men to Men Catholic Charities
716-896-6390

Forest Hill
Alternatives to Violence
718-544-2804

Howard Beach
Alternatives to Violence
718-846-2998

New City
Volunteer Counseling Services
914-634-5729

New York
Volunteer Counseling Services
914-356-4642

Alternatives to Violence
718-846-2998

Victim Services 212-577-8235

Owego
Intervention Towards Peace
607-687-6866

Platsburg
Violence Intervention Project
518-563-8206

Syracuse
Alternatives to Violence
315-425-0901

OHIO

Akron
Family Violence Treatment Program
216-762-7481

Canton
Choices for Men 216-454-3812

Melymbrosia 216-455-2145

Cincinnati
AMEND 513-221-6343

Cleveland
Batterers Intervention Program
216-443-5620

Columbus
Domestic Violence Network
800-934-9840

Lutheran Social Services
614-228-5209

Men's Domestic Violence Program
614-444-0800

Ohio Coalition on Sexual Assault
614-268-3322

Rape Education & Prevention
614-292-0479

Dayton
Batterer's Group 513-225-3197

Granville
Denison University Counseling &
Health Center 614-587-6647

Lebanon
FAS/Batterers Info. Program
513-933-2225

Lima
Urban Minority 800-567-4673

London
Madison County Hospital Mental
Health Department 614-852-1372

Mansfield
DOVE Program for Batterers
419-774-5970

Marietta
Horizons: Counseling Center
614-374-6989

New Directions 614-397-4357

New Philadelphia
Harbor House 216-364-1374

Portsmouth
Shawnee Mental Health Center
614-354-7702

Reynoldsburg
Family Counseling 614-863-6631

Wooster
Another Way 216-263-1020

Youngstown
Burdman Group 216-743-9275

Fosterville 216-759-3040

OREGON

Portland
Domestic Violence Program
503-235-3433

RHODE ISLAND

Cranston
Brother-To-Brother/Center for Non-Violence 401-946-0163

SOUTH DAKOTA

Rapid City
MAG Men Against Abuse
605-341-8676

TEXAS

Austin
Texas Council on Family Violence
800-525-1978

Tyler
Family Violence & Sexual Assault
Bulletin 903-595-6600

WASHINGTON

Olympia
White Ribbon Campaign
206-352-9686

Seattle
Center for Prevention of Sexual & Domestic Abuse 206-634-1903

Men Against Sexual Harassment (SMASH) 206-329-7946

Violence Update, School of Social Work 206-543-5640

WEST VIRGINIA

Lewisburg
Options & Changes 304-645-6322

WISCONSIN

Madison
Domestic Abuse Project, Dane County 608-233-3317

Men Stopping Rape 608-257-4444

Wisconsin Coalition Against Sexual Assault 608-257-1516

CANADA

Downsview
Catholic Family Services
416-636-9963

Halifax
Men for Change 902-422-8476

Ottawa
Men Opposed to Violence & Exploitation 613-231-5138

Toronto
Clark Institute of Psychology
416-979-6833

Easton Alliance for the Prevention of Family Violence 416-691-5212

Family Services Agency
416-586-9777

John Howard Society 416-925-4386

Metro Men Against Violence
416-932-0102

White Ribbon Campaign
416-596-1513

Willowdale
Jewish Family & Child Services
416-638-7800

Internet Resources

ACLU Criminal Justice Site   www.aclu.org/issues/criminal/hmcj.html

American Bar Association Network   www.abanet.org/

Anti-Stalking Website   www.antistalking.com/

Dept. of Justice (Bureau of Justice Statistics)   www.ojp.usdoj.gov/bjs/

Department of Justice Office for Victims of Crime
   www.ojp.usdoj.gov/ovc/

Dept. of Justice (Office of Violence Against Women)
   www.usdoj.gov/vawo/

Domestic Violence Hotlines and Resources
   www.feminist.org/911/crisis.html

Family Violence Awareness Site   www.famvi.com/

Men's Rape Prevention Project   www.mrpp.org/

National Archive of Criminal Justice Data
   www.icpsr.umich.edu/NACJD/home.html

National Center for Victims of Crime   www.nvc.org/

National Coalition Against Sexual Assault   ncasa.org/

National Coalition Against Violent Athletes   campussafety.org/NCAVA/

National Institute of Justice   www.ojp.usdoj.gov/nij/

NOVA (National Organization for Victims Assistance)
   www.try-nova.org/

Partnership Against Violence Network   www.pavnet.org/

R.A.I.N.N. (Rape Abuse Incest National Network)   www.rain.org

Security On Campus   www.securityoncampus.org/

Stalking links   www2.geocities.com/Wellesley/8827/Stalking/links.html

Stalked (stories and support)   francieweb.com/stalked/

State Stalking Laws   www.nvc.org/law/statestk.htm

The Wounded Healer Journal   idealist.com/wounded_healer/

Victim Advocacy Center   www.fiu.edu/~victimad/index.htm

Victim Services Network   www.victimservices.org/

suggested reading

Date, Acquaintance, and Stranger Rape

Brownmiller, Susan. *Against Our Will*, New York: Simon and Schuster,1975.

De Becker, Gavin. *The Gift Of Fear, and Other Survival Signals That Protect Us From Violence.* New York: Dell Publishing, 1997.

Dyer, Wayne. *Your Erroneous Zones.* Toronto, Canada: Fitzhenry and Whiteside, Ltd., 1993.

Goring, Ruth. *Date Rape.* Downers Grove, Il.: Intervarsity Press, 1996.

Landau, Elaine. *Sexual Harassment.* New York: Walker and Company, 1993.

Ledray, Linda E. *Recovering From Rape.* New York: Henry Holt and Company, 1988.

Lipman, Ira A. *How To Protect Yourself From Crime, 3rd Edition.* Chicago: Contemporary Books, 1997.

Martin, Laura. *A Life Without Fear.* Nashville: Rutledge Hill Press, 1992.

McColgan, Aileen. *The Case For Taking The Date Out of Rape.* New York: Rivers Oram Press, Division of NYU Press, 1998.

Medea, Andra and Kathleen Thompson. *Against Rape.* New York: Ferrar, Straus, Giroux, 1994.

Miller, Maryann. *Drugs and Date Rape.* Baltimore: Rosen Publishing Group, 1995.

Mufson, Susan and Rachael Krantz. *Straight Talk About Date Rape.* Checkmark Books, 1997.

Orion, Doreen. *I Know You Really Love Me: A Psychiatrist's Journal of Erotomania, Stalking, and Obsessive Love.* New York: Macmillan, 1997.

Sanday-Reeves, Peggy. *A Woman Scorned: Acquaintance Rape on Trial.* New York: Doubleday, 1996.

Viscott, David. *I Love You, Let's Work It Out.* New York: Simon and Schuster, 1987.

Warshaw, Robin. *I Never Called It Rape.* New York: Harper and Row Publishers, 1994.

Webb, Susan. *Step Forward: Sexual Harassment and the Future of Feminism.* Lanham, Md.: Rowan and Littlefield Publishers, 1998.

Williams, Mary E. *Date Rape at Issue.* San Diego: Greenhaven Press, 1998.

Winkler, Kathleen. *Date Rape: A Hot Issue.* Springfield, N.J.: Enslow Publishers, 1999.

Wiseman, Rosalind. *Defending Ourselves: A Guide To Prevention, Self Defense And Recovery From Rape.* New York: The Noonday Press, 1994.

For Men

Beneke, Timothy. *Men On Rape: What They Have to Say About Sexual Violence.* New York: St. Martin's Press, 1983.

Funk, Rus Ervin. *Stopping Rape: A Challenge For Men.* Philadelphia: New Society Publishers, 1993.

Fossum, Merle. *Men Coming Alive In Recovery.* New York: Harper/Hazelton, 1989.

Gondolf, Edward. *Man To Man: A Guide For Men in Abusive Relationships.* New York: Sulzburger and Graham, 1994

Johnson, Scott. *Man To Man—When Your Partner Says No: Pressured Sex and Date Rape.* Brandon, Vt.: Safer Society Press, 1992.

Violence

Horsfall, Jan. *The Presence Of The Past: Male Violence in the Family.* Chicago: Allen and Unwin, 1991.

Kivel, Paul. *Men's Work: How To Stop The Violence That Tears Our Lives Apart.* Center City, Mn.: Mass Market Paperback, 1992.

McKay, Matthew, Peter Rogers, and Judith McKay. *When Anger Hurts: Quieting The Storm Within.* Oakland, Ca.: New Harbinger, 1989.

Stream, Herbert, and Lucy Freeman. *Our Wish to Kill: The Murder In All Our Hearts.* New York: St. Martin's Press, 1991.

Domestic Violence

Deschner, Jeanne. *The Hitting Habit: Anger Control For Battering Couples.* New York: Free Press, 1984.

Dwight, Edgar. *I Cried You Didn't Listen: A Survivor's Expose Of The California Youth Authority.* Venice, Ca.: Abbot, Feral House, 1991.

Gelles, Richard, and Claire Pedrick Cornell. *Intimate Violence In Families.* Phoenix: Sage, 1990.

Gelles, Richard, and Murray Strauss. *Intimate Violence.* New York: Simon and Schuster, 1988.

Gillespie, Cynthia. *Justifiable Homicide: Battered Women, Self-Defense and The Law.* Columbus, Oh.: Ohio State University Press, 1989.

Miedzian, Myriam. *Boys Will Be Boys, Breaking The Link Between Masculinity and Violence.* New York: Doubleday, 1991.

Stanko, Elizabeth. *Everyday Violence: How Women and Men Experience Sexual and Physical Danger.* Kenner, La.: Pandora, 1990

Straus, Murray, Richard Gelles, and Suzanne Steinmetz. *Behind Closed Doors: Violence In The American Family.* Waxhaw, N.C.: Anchor, 1980.

For Teens

Adams, C., and J. Fay. *Nobody Told Me It Was Rape: A Parent's Guide To Talking With Teenagers About Acquaintance Rape and Sexual Exploitation.* Santa Cruz, Ca.: Network Publications, 1984.

Bandon, Alexandra. *Date Rape.* New York: Crestwood House, 1994.

Bass, E., and Davis, L. *Beginning To Heal: A First Book For Survivors of Child Sexual Abuse.* New York: Harper, 1993.

Bean, B., and S. Bennett, S. *The Me Nobody Knows: A Recovery Guide For Teenagers.* New York: Lexington Books, 1993.

Jiivanii, Ed. *In Search Of Healing.* Albuquerque, N.M.: The Survivor Press, 1993.

Parrot, Andrea. *Sexual Assault On Campus.* Lexington, Mass.: Lexington Books, 1993.

Parrot, Andrea. *Coping With Date And Acquaintance Rape.* New York: Rosen Publishing Group, 1999.

For Survivors

Maltz, W., and B. Holman. *Incest And Sexuality: A Guide To Understanding And Healing.* New York: Lexington Books, 1991.

Maltz, Wendy. *The Sexual Healing Journey: A Guide For Survivors of Sexual Abuse.* New York: HarperCollins Publishers, 1991.

Munson, L. and K. Riskin. *In Their Own Words: A Sexual Abuse Workbook For Teenage Girls.* Washington, D.C.: Child Welfare League of America, 1995.

Polese, C. *Promise Not To Tell.* New York: Beech Tree Books, 1993.

notes

1. Bureau of Justice Statistics Special Report, "Violence Against Women," Estimates from the Redesigned Survey (U.S. Department of Justice, Office of Justice Programs, Washington, D.C., August 1995).

2. Herbert Koppel, "Lifetime Likelihood of Victimization" (U.S. Department of Justice, Bureau of Justice Statistics, Washington, D.C., 1987).

3. Robin Warshaw, *I Never Called It Rape* (New York: Harper & Row Publishers, 1988).

4. Dr. Peg Ziegler, interview by the author, Atlanta, Ga., 1989.

5. E. MacFarlane and P. Hawley, "Sexual Assault: Coping with Crisis," *The Canadian Nurse* (June, 1993).

6. Warshaw, *I Never Called It Rape.*

7. Illinois Coalition Against Sexual Assault. "Acquaintance Rape Sexual Violence: Facts and Statistics" (Springfield, Il., 1994).

8. Warshaw, *I Never Called It Rape.*

9. Lawrence A. Greenfield, "Sex Offenses and Offenders—An Analysis of Data on Rape and Sexual Assault" (U.S. Department of Justice, Office of Justice Programs, Washington, D.C., February 1997).

10. The Community Epidemiology Work Group, "Epidemiologic Trends in Drug Abuse Advance Report," National Institute on Drug Abuse (June 1995).

11. Illinois Coalition Against Sexual Assault. "Acquaintance Rape Sexual Violence: Facts and Statistics" (Springfield, Il., 1994)

12. N.M. Malamuth, "Rape Proclivity Among Males," *Social Issues* (January 1981).

13. Greenfield, Sex Offenses and Offenders-An Analysis of Data on Rape and Sexual Assault.

14. Janet Bode, *Fighting Back—How To Cope With The Medical, Emotional, and Legal Consequences of Rape* (New York: MacMillan, 1978).

15. Karen S. Peterson, "Full Disclosure," *USA Today* (16 December 1994).

16. Peterson, "Full Disclosure."

17. Gordon Clay, *The National Men's Resource Calendar* (Vol. 9, No. 1, 1993).

18. Patricia Tjaden and Nancy Thoennes, "Stalking in America: Findings From the National Violence Against Women Surve" (U.S. Department of Justice, National Institute of Justice, Washington, D.C., 1998).

19. Louis Harris and Associates, Inc., "First Comprehensive National Survey of American Women Finds Them at Significant Risk," (The Commonwealth Fund, New York, 14 July 1993).

20. "The Many Faces of Domestic Violence and It's Impact on the Workplace," *Savvy Management* (New York: The Body Shop, 1998).

index

men: advice for, 173–86; agenda,
65–66; attitudes, 4–5, 16, 182;
beliefs, 67; suggested reading, 199

Men are from Mars, Women are from Venus
(Gray), 64

mental disorders, 143

Mexican Valium. *See* Rohypnol

murder, 55, 56, 61

My Sister Sam (television), 144

myth vs. fact, 176–77

N

National Coalition Against Sexual
Assault, 96

National Interfraternity Conference,
36

O

obsession, 143

Oleoresin Capsicum. *See* Pepper Spray

over-protection, 128

P

parties, 31, 34, 62

PCP, 50

Penn State University, 48

Pepper Spray, 89–91

personal ads, 8

personality disorders, 145

personality type (diagram), 52

physical abuse, 3, 22, 24, 40, 55, 56,
61. *See also* dating violence;
domestic violence

planning ahead, 30, 32

police, 104–6, 152, 168

police report, 27, 91, 102–4

popular culture, 45, 54, 142

post-traumatic stress disorder, 84,
120–22

power, 5, 58, 61, 177, 180

Power Assertive Rapist. *See* Control
Freak Rapist

Power Reassurance Rapist. *See*
Gentleman Rapist

pregnancy testing, 112

promiscuity, 119

prosecution, 44–45, 106, 123

R

R2. *See* Rohypnol

rage, 57, 117

rape: definition of, 3; emotional
response, 115–16; physical
responses, 119; suggested reading,
198–99; symptoms, 26, 114–15

rape crisis centers, 28

rape enablers, 38, 39–50

rape myth, 45–47

rape prevention, x, 3: language,
74–75, 78–79, 165, 178

Real Rape (Estrich), 83

Recovering from Rape (Ledray), 104, 115

recovery, 84

responsibility, 177, 181

restraining order, 147, 151, 168

revenge, 117

about the author

Scott Lindquist is certified through the Florida State Attorney General's Office as a Crime Prevention Practitioner and through the Georgia Crime Prevention Association as a Crime Prevention Specialist in rape prevention. He is a graduate of the Florida Crime Prevention Training Institute.

Lindquist has presented his crime prevention seminar to hundreds of thousands of people in universities such as the Southern Connecticut State University, Georgia Tech University, and the City University of New York, as well as in corporations such as AT&T, 3M Corp., American Express, and Texaco, and government agencies such as the Internal Revenue Service, the Social Security Administration, and the U.S. Federal Reserve Bank. He also has been interviewed on hundreds of television and radio stations worldwide. \

Scott Lindquist has made it his life's work to eradicate rape as an issue for American women. He is available to speak to college, university, or corporate groups, and can be reached at:

P.O. Box 71452
Marietta, Georgia 30007-1452
Phone: 770-973-1493 Fax: 770-579-0009
Email: scott-lindquist@eudoramail.com